Stuff
White
People
Like

Stuff

THE DEFINITIVE GUIDE

White

TO THE UNIQUE TASTE

People

OF MILLIONS

Like

Christian Lander

RANDOM HOUSE TRADE PAPERBACKS NEW YORK

To my mother, Jennifer,
who by nature of being born
in England granted me an ethnicity

Stuff
White
People
Like

1 Coffee

There is no doubt that white people love coffee. Yes, it's true that Asians like iced coffee and people of all races enjoy a cup. But it is a certainty that the first person at your school to drink coffee was a white person. It was obvious that they didn't enjoy it, but they did it anyway, until they liked it—like cigarettes.

As white people begin to age, a genuine taste for coffee will emerge. During this time white people will also develop a self-proclaimed "addiction." This leads to them saying things like "You do *not* want to see me before I get my morning coffee." White guys will also call it anything but coffee: "rocket fuel," "java," "joe," "black gold," and so forth. It's pretty much garbage all around.

It's worth noting that where white people buy coffee is almost as important as the drink itself. For the most part, white people love Starbucks, although they will profess to hate how the chain is now a multinational corporation. This hatred is often sublimated by their relief at seeing one in an airport. The best place for white people to drink coffee is at a locally owned coffeeshop that offers many types of drinks, free Wi-Fi, and some sort of message board that is peppered with notices about rooms for rent and bands looking for bass players.

White people are given extra points for buying Fair Trade coffee, because paying the extra $2 means they are making a difference while their peers are drinking liquid oppression.

Religions Their Parents Don't Belong To

White people will often say they are "spiritual" but not religious. This usually means that they will believe in any religion that

doesn't involve Jesus. The most popular choices include Buddhism, Hinduism, Kabbalah, and, to a lesser extent, Scientology. A few even dip into Islam, but that's much rarer, since you have to make real sacrifices and actually go to a mosque.

For the most part, white people prefer religions that produce artifacts and furniture that fit into their home or wardrobe. They are also particularly drawn to religions that do not require a lot of commitment or donations.

When a white person tells you "I'm a Buddhist/Hindu/Kabbalahist," the best thing to do is ask how they arrived at their religious decision. The story will likely involve a trip to Thailand or a college class on religion.

Film Festivals

White people can't get enough of film festivals, especially Sundance, Toronto, and Cannes. This love can be due to a number of factors.

Fact #1: 90 percent of white people have taken a film class at some point in their life.

Fact #2: White people like feeling smart without doing work—two hours in a theater is easier than ten hours with a book.

Fact #3: If white people aren't going backpacking, they generally like to travel with a specific purpose.

Fact #4: 75 percent of white people believe they either have the potential to or will become filmmakers/screenwriters/ directors at some point.

Fact #5: White people hate stuff that is "mainstream"—so they go to film festivals, where they see movies that every other person in their demographic wants to see. It's a pretty sweet way to rebel.

Fact #6: It is required by white-person law that you publicly declare foreign cinema to be better than Hollywood movies, and on par with indie film.

Fact #7: White people earn credibility by being into films from strange countries: "Oh, you liked *Sideways*? Yeah, I didn't see it, I'm really into Serbian film now. They had a great retrospective at the Vancouver Festival."

Assists

When you say the word "assist," the first thing you think about is Steve Nash and Wayne Gretzky. White people love to pass, it's no secret.

In basketball, passing is kind of a must, so that white guys can

carve out a niche and guarantee acceptance on a team. Trying to be a white guy who dunks is like trying to be a white rapper— yeah, there are a few, but you have to work twice as hard for half the results.

One explanation is that white people still feel guilty over slavery, colonialism, and the crusades, so passing is a way to make up for it. But more important, it makes them feel good to help others.

When you are a captain at a pick-up basketball game and you want to take a lot of shots, it's a good idea to pick a white guy.

Farmer's Markets

White people are drawn to farmer's markets like moths to a flame. In fact, white people have such strong instincts that if you release a white person into a random Saturday morning they will return to you with a reusable bag full of fruits and vegetables.

White people like farmer's markets for a number of reasons. The first is their undying need to support local economies and small businesses; the idea of buying direct from the farmer helps them assuage the fears instilled in them by reading *Fast Food Nation* (and yes, every white person has read this book).

Some of the other reasons include: it's outside (white people love being outdoors), they can bring their dogs and children in expensive strollers, and they get to see other white people. If they are single, it's a good place to meet other single white people who share their passion for sustainability.

If you are looking for an activity you can share with your white friends, nothing will progress the relationship faster than a trip to a farmer's market.

6 Organic Food

Because of the balance of global wealth and power, there is a general assumption that white people are pretty shrewd. And for the most part, history has proven this to be true. But white people have one great weakness: organic food.

Just as with farmer's markets, white people believe that organic food is grown by farmers who wear overalls, drive tractors, and don't use pesticides. In spite of the fact that most organic food is made by major agribusiness, which just uses it as an excuse to jack up prices, white people will always lose their mind for organic anything. Never mind the fact that if the entire world were to switch to 100 percent organic food tomorrow there would be mass starvation and famine.

White people don't care about this. As long as they aren't eating pesticides, they are pretty sure they can live forever. It's almost guaranteed that if some Colombian drug lord can start offering "organic" cocaine, he'll be the richest guy ever.

What's in That Canvas Grocery Bag?

You have probably seen white people leaving the grocery store with canvas bags. If you've ever wondered what was in those bags, here is a breakdown:

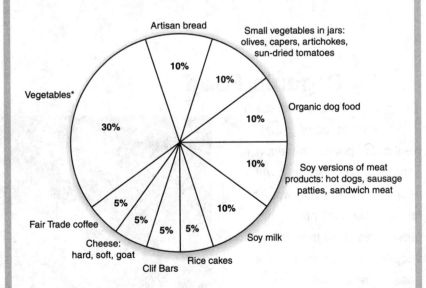

Artisan bread — 10%

Small vegetables in jars: olives, capers, artichokes, sun-dried tomatoes — 10%

Organic dog food — 10%

Soy versions of meat products: hot dogs, sausage patties, sandwich meat — 10%

Soy milk — 10%

Rice cakes — 5%

Clif Bars — 5%

Cheese: hard, soft, goat — 5%

Fair Trade coffee — 5%

Vegetables* — 30%

* Vegetables purchased at Whole Foods or an organic food co-op are considered a poor substitute for those purchased at a farmer's market. In lieu of a farmer's market, it is also acceptable to get your vegetables from an organic food delivery service.

Diversity

White people love ethnic diversity, but only as it relates to restaurants.

Many white people from cities like Los Angeles, San Francisco, and New York will spend hours talking about how great it is that they can get sushi and tacos on the same street. But they will also send their kids to private school with other rich white kids so that they can avoid the "low test scores" that come with educational diversity. It's important to note that white people do not like to be called out on this fact. It will make them feel even more guilty than they already do.

If you run an ethnic restaurant you can be guaranteed repeat business and huge tips if you act like your white customers are adventurous and cultured for eating food that isn't sandwiches or pasta. In fact, even if you do not own a restaurant, it's a good idea to congratulate white people for being adventurous eaters. It will make their year.

8   Barack Obama

White people like Barack Obama because they are afraid that if they don't they will be considered racist.

9   Making You Feel Bad for Not Going Outside

As mentioned earlier, white people love to be outside. But not everyone knows that another thing they like to do is make people

feel bad for wanting to watch sports on TV or play video games. While it would be easy to get angry at white people for this, remember it is hardwired in their heads that the greatest thing people can do in their free time is hike/walk/bike outdoors.

Usually, they will see that you are preparing to enjoy your life and they will say, "Hey, let's go for a hike in the park," and most people will say, "Hey, thanks, but I've been working all week and I'm really excited about watching this game," and then they will respond, "Don't be a lump on the couch, you're wasting your life away," etc. If you ignore them, they will eventually go away.

And, much like most things with white people, they win both ways. If you decide to go with them, they feel good about getting someone off the couch and "into the fresh air," and if you don't go, they can spend their entire time outdoors saying, "Boy, this is great, X doesn't know what he/she is missing!" and running on a mix of self-satisfaction, Odwalla juice, and muesli.

10 Wes Anderson Movies

White people love Wes Anderson movies more than they love their kids. If a white guy takes a white girl to a Wes Anderson movie on their first date, and neither of them have seen it, they will immediately commence a relationship that is reflected in songs by Ryan Adams and Bright Eyes.

Wes Anderson movies have this way of being sort of funny and a little clever, so white people in the audience will laugh like crazy. Also, if they don't get the joke and other white people start laughing, they'll all join in. It's pretty much the case that if one dude with glasses laughs, the entire theater will be in stitches within 15 seconds.

If you find yourself in a situation with a white person and an awkward silence falls over you, mention any of the movies below and you will have something to talk about, and they will like you. Here are some approved comments:

1. *The Darjeeling Limited* (2007): "Owen Wilson is just fantastic. It's so great to see that he's back."
2. *Hotel Chevalier* (2007): "Can you believe Natalie Portman got kind of naked?"
3. *The Life Aquatic with Steve Zissou* (2004): "I know a lot of people said they didn't like this film, but I thought it was fantastic." (Note: It is acceptable to be critical of this movie.)
4. *The Royal Tenenbaums* (2001): "This movie changed my life."
5. *Rushmore* (1998): "This is when Bill Murray really changed in my eyes. He's so fantastic in the movie, and Jason Schwartzman is a true star."
6. *Bottle Rocket* (1996): "I saw this movie in 1994."
   Special Entry: It is always a good idea to say that you love Wes Anderson soundtracks.

Asian Girls

Ninety-five percent of white males have, at one point in their lives, experienced yellow fever. Many factors have contributed to this phenomenon, such as guilt from head taxes, internment camps, dropping the nuclear bomb, and the Vietnam War. This exchange works both ways, as Asian girls have a tendency to go for white guys. (White girls never go for Asian guys. Bruce Lee and Paul Kariya's dad are the only recorded instances in modern history.) Asian girls often do this to get back at their strict traditional fathers. There is also the option of dating black guys, but they know deep down that this would give their non-English-speaking grandmothers a heart attack.

White men love Asian women so much that they will go to extremes like stating that Sandra Oh is sexy, teaching English in Asia, playing in a coed volleyball league, or attending institutions such as UBC (dubbed University of a Billion Chinese) or UCLA (University of CaucAsians Living among Asians). Another factor that draws white guys to Asian women is that white women are jealous of them.

Take, for instance, the fact that Asian women well into their thirties and forties retain teen or college-girl looks without the help of Botox, yoga, or a trendy diet. Asian women also avoid key white-women characteristics such as having a midlife crisis, divorce, and hobbies that don't involve taking care of the children. When white guy and Asian girl marry, they produce hybrids that are aesthetically pleasing but often very annoying. This practice is also a means by which white people can catch up to the Asian peoples in the population race, as the hybrids often act white rather than Asian.

12 Nonprofit Organizations

It is a known fact that white people make up 95 percent of nonprofit organizations. They can't get enough of them.

They like working there for a number of reasons, the most important of which is that it gives them a sense of self-importance. They can then tell their friends and parents that they are "helping" society, not just working to make money.

If a white person can stick around long enough, the nonprofit organization can eventually become a lucrative position. This is because nonprofits retain their top executives by paying a salary competitive with similar positions in other industries. So you can be working at a nonprofit and still make six figures, and you don't have accountability or pressure. White people can't lose!

13 | Tea

It is a known fact that white people consume, on average, 25 different teas in a given year.

Back in the old days, white people would go all over the world to get teas from places like India and Sri Lanka. All of a sudden, white people were into tea. But as we moved forward, white people were like, "Man, one kind of tea is not enough, we need more." And now people are into green tea, chamomile, chai, white tea, red tea, jasmine tea, oolong tea, black tea, orange pekoe, and other specialty

varieties. They are even opening stores and websites devoted to sending white people all sorts of tea.

If you find yourself in a situation with a white person, acceptable things to say include "I'm really into tea right now" or "My favorite thing is to get a nice cup of tea and curl up in a chair with a good book." But do not remind them about the role of colonialism in tea, it will make them feel sad.

Having Black Friends

Much has been made about the way that white people adore all aspects of black culture and history. These days the majority of hip-hop, jazz, blues, and African-American history fans are actually white people. Ask white people about Cornel West and they might be moved to tears of respect (very rare). So it comes as no surprise that white people love having black friends. They serve many valuable functions.

The most important role that black friends can play in white culture is that they can be used as physical evidence that white people are not racist. Did you know that if you are able to acquire a friend of every race then you are officially designated as the least racist person on earth? Though this is impossible, white people treat it the same way that Buddhists view enlightenment—unattainable, but with great virtue in the attempt.

Black friends can also be used to confirm that a white person is knowledgeable about African-American culture. Many white people are constantly striving to be recognized as experts, and many consider it a life achievement to be befriended and acknowledged by a black person. But note, do not dole out your praise like piñata candy. Once white people have achieved this goal, they will be more difficult to manipulate. So it is best to tease them with little bits of praise, balanced with a few barbs. "I have to hand it to you for putting KRS-One on that party mix. I mean, you went with a pretty well-known song, but still, good job."

Also note that all white people fantasize about being brought to an authentic "African-American" experience such as a Baptist church or a barbecue restaurant in a neighborhood that they are afraid of.

Finally, an abundance of black friends (defined in white culture as two) also enables a white person to be the resident expert on African-American issues when there are no black people around.

Moving beyond friendship, some white people actively seek out opportunities to begin romantic relationships with black people. Dating, marrying, and subsequently having a child with a black person is considered one of the greatest things a white person can do. It delivers a lifetime of opportunities to get offended and feel superior to friends with white children, but still ranks slightly behind Adopting Foreign Children (#133).

 # Yoga

Though its roots are in India, the global tree of yoga has most of its branches in rich white neighborhoods. Yoga has been so thoroughly embraced by white people because it requires large amounts of money and time, two things that white people have a lot of.

Yoga is essentially stretching with guidance. Advanced yoga is just regular yoga done in a very hot room.

You might think that since yoga is such a minimalist activity, it can be done almost anywhere. But you would be wrong. Yoga must take place on hardwood floors at a studio. Exposed beams are generally believed to enhance yoga experiences by 40 percent.

Being noncompetitive, you might think that yoga can just be done in any type of clothes that allow for a full range of motion; again you would be wrong. Yoga is much more than just an activity, it is a chance to showcase $80 pants that are tailor-made for the rigors of yoga.

And last, but not least, yoga feels exotic and foreign. It has become sort of like a religion that prizes flexibility and expensive clothes. Also, deep down, white people feel that their participation makes up for years of colonial rule in India.

16 Gifted Children

White people love "gifted" children. Do you know why? Because an astounding 100 percent of their kids are gifted! Isn't that amazing?

I'm pretty sure the last nongifted white child was born in 1962 in Reseda, California. Since then, it's been a pretty sweet run.

The way it works is that white kids who are actually smart are quickly identified as "gifted" and take special classes and eventually end up in college and then law school or med school.

But wait, aren't there white people who aren't doctors or lawyers, or even all that smart? Well, here is another of those awesome white-person win-win situations. If white kids get crappy grades and can't seem to ever do anything right in school, they are still gifted! How, you ask? They are just *too* smart for school. They are too creative, too advanced to care about the trivial minutiae of the day-to-day operations of school.

Eventually they will show their creativity in elaborate constructions of bongs and intimate knowledge of different kinds of mushrooms and hash.

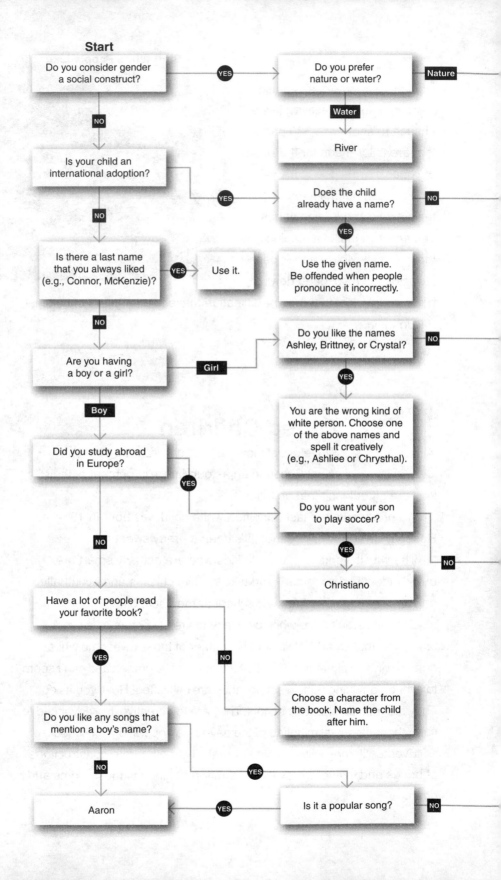

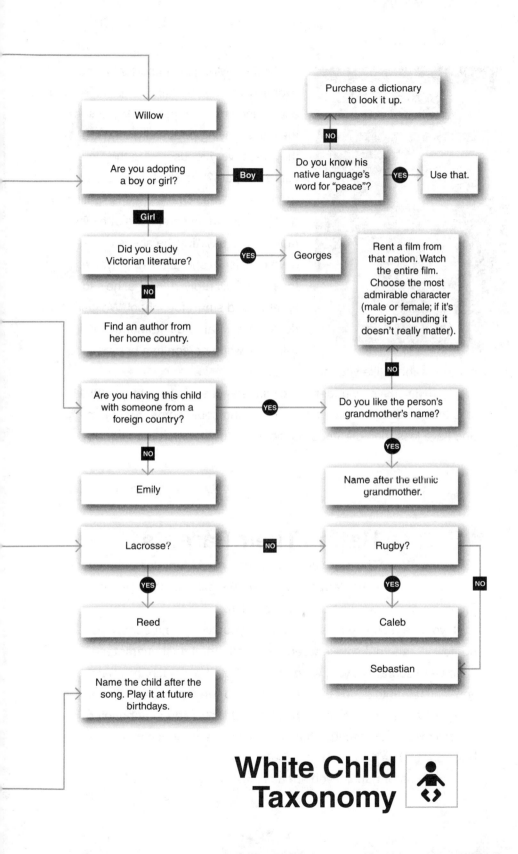

Willow

Are you adopting a boy or girl? — **Boy** → Do you know his native language's word for "peace"? — **YES** → Use that.

NO ↑ Purchase a dictionary to look it up.

Girl ↓

Did you study Victorian literature? — **YES** → Georges

NO ↓

Find an author from her home country.

Rent a film from that nation. Watch the entire film. Choose the most admirable character (male or female; if it's foreign-sounding it doesn't really matter).

NO ↑

Are you having this child with someone from a foreign country? — **YES** → Do you like the person's grandmother's name?

NO ↓

Emily

YES ↓

Name after the ethnic grandmother.

Lacrosse? — **NO** → Rugby?

YES ↓ Reed

YES ↓ Caleb

NO → Sebastian

Name the child after the song. Play it at future birthdays.

White Child Taxonomy

This knowledge is important if you ever find yourself needing to gain the acceptance of white people. If you see their kids playing peacefully, say, "Oh, they seem very focused. Are they in a gifted program?" at which point the parent will say, "Yes." Or if the kid is lighting a dog on fire while screaming at his/her mother, you say, "My, he/she is a creative one. Is he/she gifted?" To which the parent will reply, "Oh, yes, he's too creative and smart for school. We just don't know what to do." Either situation will put a white person in a better mood and make them like you more.

WARNING: *Never* under any circumstances imply that their child is less than a genius. The idea that something could come from them and have less than greatness is too much for them to bear.

 Hating Their Parents

This topic ties into a number of other items, but there is no denying that white people hate their parents. There is nothing you can do to prevent this.

If you are a strict parent who makes your kid have a curfew, do homework, and not smoke weed, then you are almost guaranteed to have them scream at you, write poems about how much they hate you, and relate to songs by bands from Orange County and Florida. Eventually, they forgive you and thank you for the tough upbringing, but still resent you because their high school experience wasn't a carbon copy of *The O.C.* or *My So-Called Life.*

On the other hand, if you are a super-laid-back parent who lets your kid go to parties and drink in the house, and you smoke weed together, you are only delaying the hatred. Because these kids eventually end up doing something stupid with their lives—dropping out of college, trying to become a painter, or spending time in a Thai prison. At which point, they hate you for being too lax and not caring enough.

But note that this hatred can be used for gain. White people love to talk about how much they hate their parents, so if you are in a situation where you need to gain a white person's trust, ask about their parents. But under no circumstances should you try to one-up them, regardless of whether or not you were an orphan, were abused, or watched your parents get shot. If you bring this up, the white person will never talk to you about their problems again, and your chances for friendship will be ruined.

18 | Awareness

An interesting fact about white people is that they firmly believe all of the world's problems can be solved through "awareness"—meaning the process of making other people aware of problems, magically causing someone else, like the government, to fix it.

This belief allows them to feel that sweet self-satisfaction without actually having to solve anything or face any difficult challenges, because the only challenge of raising awareness is getting the attention of people who are currently unaware.

What makes this even more appealing for white people is that you can raise "awareness" through expensive dinners, parties, marathons,

T-shirts, fashion shows, concerts, and bracelets. In other words, white people just have to keep doing stuff they like, *except* that now they can feel better about making a difference.

Raising awareness is also awesome because once you raise awareness to an acceptable though arbitrary level, you can just back off and say, "Bam! Did my part. Now it's your turn. Fix it."

So, to summarize: you get all the benefits of helping (self-satisfaction, telling other people) but no need for difficult decisions or the ensuing criticism. (How do you criticize awareness?) Once again, white people find a way to score that sweet double victory.

Popular things to be aware of: the environment, diseases like cancer and AIDS, Africa, poverty, anorexia, homophobia, middle school field hockey/lacrosse teams, drug rehab, and political prisoners.

International Travel

White-person travel can be broken into two categories—First World and Third World.

First World is Europe and Japan, and man, this travel is not only beloved but absolutely essential in the development of a white person. Every white person takes at least one trip to Europe between the ages of 17 and 29. During this time they are likely to wear a backpack, stay at a hostel, meet someone from Ireland/Sweden/Italy with whom they have a memorable experience, get drunk, see some old churches, and ride a train.

What's amazing is that all white people have pretty much the same experience, but all of them believe theirs to be the first of its kind, so much so that they return to North America with ideas of writing novels and screenplays about it.

Upon returning home, they will also find an affinity for a particular beer or liquor from a country they visited. They use this as an excuse to mention their travels when at a bar. "Oh, I'll have a Czechznlishiyush Pilsner. You see, that was my favorite beer when I was traveling through Slovenia and the Czech Republic."

The second type of white-person travel is Third World. This is when they venture to Thailand, Africa, or South America. Some do it so that they can one-up the white people who only go to Europe. As with Europe, white people like to believe they are the first white people to make this trip. As such, they should be recognized as special and important individuals.

That's right, by going to a country, riding around on a bus or train, staying at a hotel or hostel, and eating, they are doing something important for the world.

If you are someone who lives in a country that white people like to visit, there are some things you can do for personal gain, the best of which is to make them feel fantastic by saying how you've never seen a white person before, and that you are amazed by their iPod—"A device that plays many songs? Impossible!" They might give it to you, then you can sell it for profit. Repeat as necessary.

White Globetrotter

Instructions: Fill in and have fun!

Hey everyone!

Sorry for the mass email, but I only have a short period of time

at the internet cafe here in _____.
                                    FOREIGN COUNTRY

The flight from _____ took forever, and I was
                        CITY

seated next to this really gross person from _____
                                                    COUNTRY

who wouldn't shut up. I swear, next time I fly to _____
                                                    FOREIGN COUNTRY

I'm flying first class.

So when I got to the airport I picked up my backpack and went

through Customs. I don't care what anyone tells you, it's really

not that bad unless you are carrying _____.
                                            DRUG

Speaking of which, I met this crazy _____ dude at the
                                            NATIONALITY

hostel who said he can get that for _____ an ounce!
                                        DOLLAR AMOUNT

Can you believe that?

So day one, I went on a tour of the city to visit all sorts of

_____. It was amazing, I have never felt so spiri-
   RELIGIOUS BUILDINGS

tual. I took a lot of pictures on my _____. When I get
                                        CAMERA BRAND/MODEL

back home, I am totally going to convert to _____.
                                                RELIGION OR FOOD LIFESTYLE

I can't believe it's taken me so long to discover it. Sure it will

probably freak out my parents, but I don't care.

On the way back to the hostel, I ran into some local children

who asked me all sorts of questions. I bought them some

_____ and gave them my _____, it
         SWEETS   WESTERN PRODUCT

felt so good to give back. I know they'll remember me forever. I

think they had never seen a white person before!

The next day, me and _____ from Germany con-

NAME

vinced this guy with a car to take us to a _____.

BUILDING

We had an incredible drive and the guy told us all about the his-

tory of _____. I think everyone should be forced to

FOREIGN COUNTRY

travel instead of taking history classes. You just learn so much

more when you actually experience history instead of just read-

ing about it in some book. Anyway, when we got there, it was

just us and no tourists. I wish all of you could have seen it. I

know it's cliché but I would describe the _____

BUILDING

as truly _____.

CLICHÉ

The very next day, a few of us at the hostel decided to get

_____. It was so cheap, we spent the whole day in the

DRUG OR ALCOHOL

hostel just watching _____, which we got on

MOVIE

bootleg DVD for like a buck. After that we _____

VERB FOR INGESTING

some more and listened to _____ while talking

REGGAE ARTIST

about life and religion. We literally saw the sun come up. It was

intense.

Wish all you guys were here.

_____!

FOREIGN EXPRESSION

20 | Being an Expert on *Your* Culture

White people are pretty conflicted about their culture. On one hand, they are proud of the art, literature, and film produced by white culture. But on the other, they are very ashamed of all the bad things about white culture: the KKK, colonialism, slavery, Jim Crow laws, feudalism, and the treatment of Native Americans.

One way they can make up for the shame is by becoming marginally acquainted with foreign cultures. It is generally acceptable for a white person to learn a few terms in a language spoken primarily by nonwhites (such as Chinese, Tagalog, or Portuguese). They can then use these phrases to order certain "more authentic" dishes in restaurants.

White people can also take passing interest in film, politics, music, or art from these cultures. When they actually meet someone from that culture, or at least who has parents from that culture, they cannot wait to engage you in all the details that they have learned. "Have you heard the new Andy Lau CD? It's awesome!"

It is imperative that you recognize how special and unique this white person is for knowing about your culture. Acceptable responses include "Wow, I've never seen a white person order chicken feet" or "How did you find out about that film? I didn't think they had dubbed/subtitled it yet."

These responses will fill white people with that self-satisfaction they need. Also, the responses serve as reminders that they are not racist, which also makes them feel terrific.

21 | Writer's Workshops

It's no secret: White people want to be writers. Why wouldn't they? They could work 10 hours a week from a country house in Maine or New England, get called a genius by other white people, and maybe get a book made into a film. Every single white person harbors this dream. No matter what they tell you, all of them have at least one chapter of a novel or memoir stashed away somewhere.

Being a marginally crafty race, white people will often seek out every possible route to achieving this goal, and one of the most popular methods has been writer's workshops. These are expensive mini go-to-school-type vacations where you talk with a published writer (often someone you haven't heard of, but they have a book on Amazon) who will tell you how they became a writer. If there is time, they will listen to you read your stuff and tell you that it's good but it needs work on (a) structure, (b) characters, or (c) dialogue. Then they will collect their check and go back to their country house or studio apartment in New York.

22 | Having Two Last Names

In recent years, white people have loved giving their children two last names. This is a direct result of white women thinking it's sexist and outdated to take their husband's name.

It is also sexist that the child would carry the name of only one parent, especially since the unnamed parent is the one who carried the child

for nine months. The only logical solution is to give the kid a split last name. White people can't get enough of it!

As a result, we have children growing up named Elijah Sadler-Moore.

While it's true that many Spanish-speaking cultures do this, oftentimes their names are crazy long but are shortened into sweet one-word nicknames like Pele. Also, there is a historical precedent.

As this is a recent phenomenon, we have yet to see what happens when one split-named person marries another split-named person. Does their kid end up with four last names?

There are some concerns that collegiate lacrosse and soccer jerseys are going to look pretty strange in the next few years.

Microbreweries

White people don't like stuff that's easy to acquire. Beer is no exception.

They generally try to avoid beers like Budweiser, Labatt's, Molson, Coors, and Heineken because if it's mass-produced it is bad. Pabst Blue Ribbon is given a pass because it doesn't advertise, has a cool can, and is one of the cheapest beers around. When white people are young they like to say how much they like Pabst because they can't afford anything else, then say it tastes great. If you want to make a white person laugh when they bring up Pabst, just say, "You know, they only give the Blue Ribbon to first place . . . even if it was handed out in 1893."

But Pabst is most definitely the exception and not the rule.

When white people need a beer, they turn to microbreweries, which seem to be located almost exclusively in New England, California, Oregon, Quebec, and Colorado. Being able to walk into a bar and order a beer that no one has heard of makes white people feel good about their refined beer palate.

A friend of mine once met a white guy who brought a notebook with him to every bar. He would then keep a record of all the beers he drank and his experience with them. He called it his "beer journal."

Also of note: Most white people want to open a microbrewery at some point. One that uses organic hops.

24 Wine

There are a lot of cultures that like wine, but the way white people like wine is on a whole different level.

Within white culture, you are expected to know what a good wine is, what wine is not acceptable to like, and the names of prominent wine-growing regions. But because there are thousands of wineries, thousands of wines, and a limited time to try them or learn about the subject, white people often need to fake knowledge. If they are exposed as not being knowledgeable, they will look like fools and their peers will consistently make jokes about them liking Boone's Farm, Thunderbird, Wild Irish Rose, or Cisco. This humiliation can crush a white person for years.

When a white person offers you wine, you take a small sip and then say, "Ooh, that's nice. What country is it from?" Then they will say the name of the country and you say, "I love wines from that country, I would love to get a villa in the wine region there." White people will nod

in agreement as they all want to have a second home in a wine region like Napa, Tuscany, or Santa Barbara.

It is also a good idea to say that your favorite wine is from a small winery called [make up a name like Spotswood, Red Duck, or a random Spanish-sounding name] in [Australia, Argentina, France, California, or Chile] that is hard to find in whatever country you are in. White people will be impressed that they have not heard of this wine and will consider you to be a very smart person. They will also make a note to try to find that wine, and when they can't find it, your status will rise even higher.

Wines that are acceptable: red, white (less so).

Wines that are unacceptable (unless to be consumed in an ironic fashion): white Zinfandel, wine in a box, rosé, fortified wine, Arbor Mist, Chinese cooking wine.

25 David Sedaris

For many of you, this item will be confusing, as you will be wondering who exactly this David Sedaris is. He is a humorist who writes for *The New Yorker* and has several books, including *Barrel Fever* and *Holidays on Ice*.

His stuff is kind of funny, but white people go crazy and will pay hundreds of dollars to hear him read from his own book. Let me say that again: they will pay money to see someone read from a book they have already read. They know the jokes are coming, they know the punch lines, but they feel the need to hear the author actually say them.

White people universally love David Sedaris, so if they ever ask you, "Who are your favorite authors?" you should always reply, "David Sedaris." They will instantly launch into a story about how much they love his work, and the conversation will go from there, and you won't have to talk about books anymore. This is also safer than saying Jonathan Franzen, Dave Eggers, or Shakespeare. White people are very divided on these authors and might actually ask you questions about why you like them. Stick with David Sedaris and

you can't lose! If they do press you, just say, "I read a lot, and I never laugh out loud when I read, but Sedaris is just brilliant."

This advice will make white people respect you, trust you, and be more willing to invite you to their parties.

White Annotated Bibliography

Dave Eggers, *A Heartbreaking Work of Staggering Genius* "Honestly, I'm not afraid to call this the book of our generation. He captures all that we are and aspire to be."

Jonathan Safran Foer, *Everything Is Illuminated* "The book is incredible. The accented English literally jumps off the page and demands to be read out loud."

Michael Chabon, *The Amazing Adventures of Kavalier & Clay* "His first book was good, but I think he really comes into his own as an author with this novel. It does this amazing job of combining all that I remember loving about comic books with all that I love about prose fiction."

Henry James, all books "If you send me to a desert island, just make sure I have a page of James's delicate prose in my back pocket. I promise you it can keep me entertained and thinking for months."

All Victorian novels "So your favorite books are *Pride and Predjudice*, *Wuthering Heights*, and *Vanity Fair*? Convenient that they've all been turned into movies, don't you think?"

Michael Pollan, *The Omnivore's Dilemma* "The politics of food are fascinating, and this book will change the way you eat and the way you think forever."

James Joyce, *Finnegans Wake* "I love Joyce, although I feel as though *Dubliners* captures the spirit of the Irish more than this book." (Note: It is an old white-person trick to steer conversation away from books that you have not read.)

William S. Burroughs, *Junky* "Did you like *Trainspotting*? Yeah, well, Burroughs was doing that in 1960 with this book." (Note: Do not bring up *Naked Lunch*; white people don't even pretend to understand it.)

Jack Kerouac, *On the Road* "I read this book when I was sixteen years old. I would say that by the time I reached page 2, I knew I wanted to be a writer." (Note: Advanced white people are disgusted by people who like this book.)

Chuck Palahniuk, *Lullaby* "You know, I've never even read *Fight Club*. I find his other works to be far more engaging."

Nick Hornby, *How to Be Good* "I fell in love with Hornby when I read *High Fidelity* in 1995, and I think he gets better with each book. This one is my absolute favorite though."

Jay McInerney, *Bright Lights, Big City* Note: This novel is written in second person ("You step outside," etc.). This makes it very easy to test if a white person has actually read it or just watched the movie starring Michael J. Fox.

Bret Easton Ellis, *American Psycho* "Reading Ellis is like watching an amazingly melodramatic soap opera and then realizing that it actually taught you something at the end. I can't tell you how much time I really spent thinking, just thinking, after reading this book."

David Foster Wallace, *Infinite Jest* "Did you know that this book is more than 1,000 pages long? I read it in high school, on spring break. A thousand pages."

Marcel Proust, *Remembrance of Things Past* "I hope to read this one day." (Note: Any person who has actually read all fifteen volumes has a graduate degree in English.)

Manhattan (and Now Brooklyn, Too!)

Oftentimes if you ask white people about where to travel, you will get a lot of responses. But if you ask them about New York, white people will go nuts. They love the city universally and either live there, have lived there, will live there, or want to live there.

White people like New York because it has artists, restaurants, a subway, history, diversity, plays, and other white people. It literally has everything white people need to thrive! The only thing it's missing is nature, but Central Park is right there, and since you are walking all the time, you are outside!

If you are from New York, mention it to a white person. They will be instantly fascinated and start asking questions. When they inevitably tell you what they know about your hometown ("I know this great Italian place . . ."), you should respond by saying, "Man, I thought only New Yorkers knew about that spot."

Another secret fact about white people: if you are in a group setting and the topic of New York City comes up, find the highest-ranking white person and say, "Oh, are you from New York?" To them, this means you are calling them cultured, cool, and urban. They will respond with something like, "Oh, well, I've spent a lot of time there" or "I lived there for three months." You will have instantly become popular.

27 Marathons

In life, there are certain milestones of physical activity that can define you: a 40-yard dash in under 5 seconds, a 40-inch vertical leap, and so forth. To a white person, the absolute pinnacle of fitness is to run a marathon. Not to win, just to run.

White people will train for months, telling everyone who will listen about how they get up early in the morning, how they run when it rains, how it makes them feel so great and gives them energy.

When they finish the marathon, they will generally take a photo of themselves in a pair of New Balance sneakers and running shorts, with their marathon number held in both hands over their head in tri-

umph. (Seriously, look it up, this is universal.)

They will then set goals like running in the Boston Marathon or the New York City Marathon.

If you find yourself in a situation where a white person is talking about a marathon, you must be impressed or you will lose favor with them immediately. Running for a certain length of time on a specific day is a very important thing to a white person and should not be demeaned.

Also worth noting: the more competitive white people prefer triathlons because Kenyans can't afford $10,000 specialty bicycles. If the subject ever comes up, just say that triathletes are in better shape than football and basketball players. It's not true, but it will make the conversation a lot more genial.

28 Not Having a TV

The number-one reason white people like not having a TV is so that they can tell you that they don't have a TV.

On those lonely nights when white people wish they could be watching *American Idol, Lost,* or *Grey's Anatomy,* they comfort themselves by thinking of how when people talk about the show tomorrow they can say, "I didn't see it, I don't have a TV. That stuff rots your brain." It is effective in making other white people feel bad, and making themselves feel good about their life and life choices.

These people often fill their time by talking to other friends who don't watch TV about how they don't watch TV, looking at leaves, cooking, reading books about left-wing politics, and going to concerts/protests/poetry slams.

Generally, this makes them very boring and gives you very little to talk to them about. It's important that you *never* suggest they are making a mistake or that there is value to owning a TV. You should just try to steer the conversation to allow them to talk about how they are better than you.

'80s Night

If you ever find yourself wanting to take your relationship with white people to the next level, one of the best places to meet a potential partner is at any '80s-night event in your local city.

White people cannot get enough of '80s music, partly out of nostalgia and partly since it was the last time that pop music wasn't infused with hip-hop or R 'n' B stylings. Artists like Joy Division, New Order, and Elvis Costello were all pretty well respected and had solid runs at the charts. Also, less respected artists like Wham, Rick Astley, and Cameo are still easy for white people to dance to.

If you are in a social situation and wish to turn it into one more conducive for romance, you should always ask, "Does anyone know a club with a good '80s night?" at which point you will be flooded with suggestions and invitations to dance to Debbie Gibson songs.

Wrigley Field

One of the best things someone can do to gain the respect and trust of a white person is to attend a baseball game with them at Wrigley Field, the home of the Chicago Cubs. In addition to being one of the favorite baseball teams of white people (after the Boston Red Sox), the stadium is viewed as a must visit for virtually all white people regardless of their concern for the actual Cubs.

There are rumors that Wrigley Field is like that device in *The Fly* that turned Jeff Goldblum into a bug, except that instead of turning a

human into an insect, it can turn nonwhite people into white people. The best evidence of this comes from the '80s TV show *Perfect Strangers,* in which the foreigner Balki Bartokomous needed only to attend one game at the famed field to join his cousin Larry as a white person.

So why do white people love it so much? The biggest reason is that white people love historical buildings. This is because they are reminded of the olden days, when everything was made out of brick and ethnic mothers yelled out windows at their children to stop playing stickball and come in for dinner. Wrigley is a reminder of days gone by, although it is unwise to point out that white people are being nostalgic for an era when baseball was only played by white people. It will make them feel sad and will likely ruin their expensive "bleacher" seats.

White people also enjoy the neighborhood around Wrigley Field, as it is filled with old houses, "character," and white people. This cannot be understated, as the Chicago White Sox used to play in the oldest stadium in the league, but because of its location on the South Side, it didn't have quite the same appeal to generations of white college students.

A trip to Wrigley Field with a white person can be the final piece in the friendship puzzle. Be sure to bring khaki shorts, which are required for entry to the stadium.

Snowboarding

During the winter months, one of the favorite leisure activities of white people is snowboarding. The sport was invented in the '80s when a group of white people took a single ski, made it wider, and turned it sideways.

Like all other popular white activities, snowboarding requires the purchase of a lot of very expensive equipment and activity-specific clothing. Assuming that you can wear any winter jacket when you go snowboarding is a common mistake that can lead to wealthy white children laughing at you from the chairlift.

To properly snowboard, you are expected to purchase an oversized brand-name jacket and baggy snow pants. These will not be cheap. Remember, you are rebelling against the conformity of skiing, and the best way to do it is to dress exactly like everyone else.

The sport is also essential to older white people who need to show their other old white friends that they are cool.

Now that you have spent almost $2,000 for equipment and cloth-ing, you will have to pay upwards of $80 for a lift ticket. Then, following a morning of falling down, you can replenish your energy by purchasing a $14 hamburger at the snack bar. If you are lucky enough to live within a reasonable driving distance of the resort, your final expense

will be fuel costs to return home. Otherwise you can expect to pay a few hundred dollars for a room near the mountain.

In other words, a white invitation to go snowboarding is like them handing you a bill for three grand. The best response to one of these invitations is to say that you will accompany them to the mountain when a nonwhite person wins the X Games or a gold medal in the Winter Olympics.

32 Veganism/Vegetarianism

As with many white-people activities, being vegan/vegetarian enables them to feel as though they are helping the environment *and* it gives them a sweet way to feel superior to others. For further evidence, note how the vegetarian world has increasing levels of extremism (no meat, no dairy, no eggs, no fish, nothing that has been cooked, etc.).

Much like not watching TV, being vegan/vegetarian makes white people pretty hard to deal with on a day-to-day basis—having dinner, going to restaurants, and having them over to watch political debates all become major challenges as white people will talk about how they cannot eat anything and would rather that the meat and cheese be thrown in the garbage than put into their bodies.

But wait, aren't there white people who eat organic, grain-fed, free-range cattle and chicken? Yes, but these white people are racked with guilt knowing that they are still eating a dead animal, contributing to rainforest deforestation and global warming.

Whether you are dealing with a meat eater or a vegan/vegetarian, there are many ways to use this information to your advantage. If you require a favor from a vegetarian white person, you should invite them to dinner with your family. When your mother/grandmother offers them a dish with meat in it, they will reject it, saying that they are vegetarian. When the meal is over, tell them that your mom is very embarrassed, and that in your culture rejecting food is the equivalent of spitting on someone's grave. They will then owe you a favor, which can be called in when you need a trip to the airport, someone to help you move, a small interest-free loan, or a place for your friend to crash.

If you need to gain leverage with meat eaters, it's pretty easy. They already feel guilty; just point it out.

33 | Marijuana

People from many cultures (Southeast Asia, Jamaica, India, Morocco, Mexico, etc.) like marijuana, but white people take it to an entirely new level.

To simply purchase, roll, and smoke marijuana is not enough for white people. They need to make sure they know all the different strains, cultivation techniques, and methods for smoking it. They even have an entire magazine devoted to it, one that actually has centerfolds of plants that people have grown.

White people are also willing to spend more than $500 on smoking devices just to find new and more expensive ways to smoke weed.

It is worth noting that every white person, at some point, has written a high school or college paper about the history of how the DuPont company helped make weed illegal. This paper also teaches about how hemp can be used to fuel cars, make clothing, create food, cure cancer, and solve every single problem on earth.

While you would assume that most white people smoke weed between the ages of 14 and 28 (and act as though they are the first generation to have done so), the

reality is that white people smoke weed well into old age. They also smoke weed with their kids! This is not a joke. White people love weed so much that they consider it a "gift" to share with their kids. This has led to a generation that was not allowed to watch *Power Rangers* but was allowed to toke up.

All white people believe marijuana should be legalized, and they consider the Netherlands a pinnacle of enlightenment. Also, every white person has had their most profound weed-smoking experience in Amsterdam, so it's a good idea to fabricate a story about your own experience there so you can quickly forge a bond. Traditional tales use the following words: hostel, brownie, girl/guy from Hungary, crazy, locked out, chill dudes from Ireland.

Under *no circumstances* should you ever imply that people just smoke weed to get high (they do it for medical/spiritual/social reasons, etc.), or that there are any negative consequences. This will likely alienate you from white people.

On the plus side, white people are always looking for higher-quality, more potent, more organic marijuana. If you promise to hook them up with a special selection from your home country, they will likely pay a high premium.

34 Architecture

If you ask white people what they love about cities they don't live in, they will say "restaurants," "culture," and "architecture." They just can't get enough of old buildings or ultra-modern buildings next to old buildings.

If you want to fit in with white people you need to learn about I. M. Pei, Frank Lloyd Wright, Frank Gehry, and a whole swath of others. Also, be prepared to say "Bauhaus" a lot.

Once you have the basics down, you should choose a city that people are unlikely to have visited, then make up a name and choose one of the following: (a) opera house, (b) museum, (c) city hall, (d) civic center. Then put it all together into something like this: "Gehry is good, but I'm much more into the work of D. F. Winterhausen. He designed the new opera house in Podgorica." Wait for a beat and then say, "In Montenegro. Have you never been?" The white person will be left in stunned silence, reverence, and respect.

The reason white people love architecture so much is that deep down they believe they could have been great architects. They feel the same way about other professions, including professor, writer, and politician.

Also of note: White people love big books about architecture. So if you need to get one a gift, this always goes over well because it makes them feel smart without having to read too much.

35 The Daily Show with Jon Stewart / The Colbert Report

The Daily Show/Colbert Report are held in such high regard by white people that to criticize them would be the equivalent of setting the pope on fire in Italy in 1822. It just isn't done; in fact, it couldn't even be considered!

White people love to make fun of politics, especially right-wing politics. It's a pretty easy target and makes for some decent humor. But what's interesting is that white people are actually starting to believe that these two shows are legitimate news sources. "Oh, I don't watch

the news," they will say. "I watch *The Daily Show* and *The Colbert Report.* You know, studies show that viewers of those shows are more educated than people who watch Fox News or CNN."

White women all consider Jon Stewart to be the most perfect man on the planet. This is not a debate, it is law.

The Daily Show also features guests like John McCain, writers, policy analysts, and actors. It is comforting for white people to see boring celebrities get interviewed in a funny fashion. It fills their need to do something productive, but also not to work that hard at it.

Take note that Tuesday through Friday during the working week, you can break *all* awkward silences with white people by saying, "Did you see *The Daily Show/Colbert Report* last night?" At which point they will start talking until you are ready to move on to more interesting activities.

Brunch

When Loverboy sang "Everybody's working for the weekend," they meant that you work all week so that you can earn a break and go to some sweet bars or concerts and rock out as hard as possible because you have two days for the hangover to fix itself. Well, white people work for the weekend, except that their only goal is to eat brunch on Saturday or Sunday at one of their favorite breakfast places.

These places are restaurants that specialize in breakfast food and are usually only open from 8:00 A.M. to 2:00 P.M., and if you arrive at any time after 9:30, prepare to wait for up to an hour with white people who cannot wait to get vegan pancakes, eggs benedict, waffles, or deluxe French toast.

To a white person, there is no better way to spend a Saturday morning than to get up late, around 9:30, pile into the Audi or Volvo, and drive to one of these little places and eat brunch with friends. Often these brunches last for an hour or more (hence the long lines and wait times). Some white people take it to the next level and bring their dog, a newspaper, or even a laptop.

If you plan on dealing with white people, it will serve you well to know some local brunch places. This will also come in handy if you pick someone up at '80s night. In white-person law, if you meet someone at '80s night and then go out for brunch the next morning, you are automatically in a relationship. There are no exceptions.

37 Renovations

All white people are born with a singular mission in life in order to pass from regular whitehood into ultra-whitehood. Just as Muslims have to visit Mecca, all white people must eventually renovate a house before they can be complete.

Of course, most white people do not reach this goal until they are 35 or older. But the need to do it is as instinctual as walking. But it is important to note that white people have little or no interest in renovating a suburban home built after 1960 (except in Southern California). All white people dream about buying an older property ("with character") in a city, and then renovating it so the insides look all modern, with a stainless-steel fridge.

Though the seed is planted from birth, it really starts to grow when renovations take place in a family home during childhood. They don't understand why there are so many men with mustaches in their kitchen, but they know that the men will be gone in a few weeks, leaving behind a nicer kitchen and a happier mommy/daddy/life partner of parent.

Please note that *all* white people went through a renovation when they were kids. This is a good subject to bond over, perhaps with a story about how you were embarrassed at a sleepover when a friend went to the bathroom and there was a contractor on the toilet. Embellish as necessary.

Arrested Development

Even though most white people prefer to say that they don't watch TV, one thing they agree on is that *Arrested Development* was the best show ever. They love it so much!

They love it for a number of reasons. First, since the show was canceled before it jumped the shark, it's effectively like a rocker who dies at 27. Also, the show got terrible ratings, meaning that it wasn't "mainstream," which makes white people love it universally. Other examples of shows like this are *Twin Peaks* and *The Ben Stiller Show.*

They also love it because the show likes to make references to popular culture, and if there is one thing that white people love, it's cultural references that they understand (see *Garden State, The Onion,* and *Juno* for examples).

If you are ever at a white person's house and you see an orange box in their DVD collection, you should say, "Oh, you have *Arrested Development.* I love that show!" To which you will be offered a glass of wine, and perhaps an invitation to '80s night.

Also of note: The hip-hop group Arrested Development is also loved by white people.

Netflix

We all know white people love film festivals, but what about movies that don't make it to a film festival, or weren't in the local film festival? How do you get access? Thankfully, white people have Netflix.

If you don't know, Netflix sends you DVDs in the mail, and you get new ones when you send the old ones back.

White people are absolutely crazy for Netflix because all of them are convinced that there is a global conspiracy to keep good, independent, groundbreaking films from mainstream distribution (multiplexes, Blockbuster, etc.). To them, Netflix (in spite of being a for-profit company) is a brand-new way for independent filmmakers to find an audience. By subscribing, white people believe that they are changing the film industry, supporting innovation, and contributing to a cultural revolution in film.

If you see a group of white people and you need to break into the conversation, a good thing to say is "Hey, is anyone else thinking that Netflix shipping is getting slower? I'm doing this P. T. Anderson thing, and I'm only up to *Magnolia*! What's that all about?" They will relate, and talk about their own Netflix queues and how they are trying to get caught up on French New Wave.

Typical White-Person DVD Rack

Mulholland Dr. "Lynch at his finest. It took me awhile to figure this one out. I have a theory . . . but it would take me about an hour to explain it."

Donnie Darko "The most underrated film of all time."

Rashomon "Oh, you liked *Run Lola Run*? Watch this one first. Kurosawa is God."

Sixteen Candles "If you don't love John Hughes, I don't want to know you."

Pulp Fiction "I saw this in theaters three times. It made me want to be a film-maker."

Clerks "Did you know the rights to the songs cost more than the film?" (White people love movie trivia.)

Juno "The character of Juno reminds me of me."

Fight Club "I'm amazed this film was done by a big studio."

Memento "I love the play on traditional narrative."

Apocalypse Now "I read *Heart of Darkness* by Conrad before watching this film."

Garden State "Portman, great soundtrack, a real message? Sign me up."

A Clockwork Orange "Kubrick's masterpiece is as true today as it was back then. Ahead of his time."

Monty Python and the Holy Grail "You should watch this with me sometime, I can recite the whole thing. Word for word!"

Apple Products

It is surprising that it took all the way to #40 to call out Apple products. Truthfully, it might be more productive to devote the entire 40s to the various Apple products that integrate into a white person's life.

Plain and simple, white people don't just like Apple, they love Apple and need it to operate.

On the surface, you would ask yourself how white people could love a multibillion-dollar company with manufacturing plants in China and mass production, and that contributes to global pollution through the manufacture of consumer electronic devices. The simple answer: Apple products tell the world you are creative and unique. They are an exclusive product line only used by every white college student, designer, writer, English teacher, and hipster on the planet.

You see, a long time ago Macs were superpopular among layout artists and graphic designers. Then Apple released Final Cut Pro, and it became the standard for film editors. As a result, lots of creative industries used Apple computers instead of PCs. Eventually, people started making the connection, and all of a sudden all white people need to have a Mac.

When you ask white people about Macs they will say, "Oh, it's so much better than Windows," "It's just easier to use," "They are so cutting edge," and so forth. What's amazing is that white people *need* to meet people who use Windows to justify themselves spending an extra $500 for a pretty-looking machine.

It is also important that white people are reminded of their creativity; remember, you need a Mac to creatively check email, creatively check websites, and creatively watch DVDs on planes.

White people also need iPods, iPhones, Apple TV, AirPort, and anything else that Apple will produce, because they need to express their uniqueness by purchasing everything that a publicly traded company produces.

Apple products also come with stickers. Some people put them on their computers, some people put them on windows, but to take this to the pinnacle of whiteness, you need to put the Apple sticker in the rear window of your Prius, Jetta, BMW, Subaru 4WD station wagon, or Audi. You then need to drive to a local coffeeshop (Starbucks will do in a pinch) and set up your Apple for the world to see. Thankfully, the Apple logo on the back will light up! So even in a dark place, people can see how unique and creative you (and the five other people next to you doing the exact same thing) truly are!

Knowledge of Apple products can be useful in a number of social situations. If you see a white person with a Mac, an easy way to approach them is to say, "Is that a Powerbook? What OS do you have?" They will happily start talking to you, and after the requisite five minutes you can invite them to a screening of a documentary.

Indie Music

If you want to understand white people, you need to understand indie music. As mentioned before, white people hate anything that's "mainstream" and are desperate to find things that are more genuine, unique, and reflective of their experiences.

Fortunately, they have independent music.

A white person's iPod (formerly CD collection) is not merely an assemblage of music that they enjoy. It is what defines them as a person. They are always on the lookout for the latest hot band that no one has heard of, so that one day they can hit it just right and be into a band *before* it is featured in an Apple commercial. To a white person,  being a fan of a band before it gets popular is one of the most important things they can do with their life. They can hold it over their friends forever!

Indie music also produces a lot of concerts, at which white people can meet other white people. Concerts are useful, because if white people are attending the same concert, it means they both like the artist and can easily strike up a conversation that will flow from band at the show → other bands they like → where they went to/go to school → where to get the best vegan food in town → agreement to meet at said restaurant for awkward date.

It is worth noting that white people are expected to stay current with music and go to concerts well into their forties. Unlike at dance or hip-hop clubs, there are few stigmas attached to being the "old guy at the club."

WARNING: Indie music is perhaps the most dangerous subject you can discuss with white people. One false move and you will lose their respect and admiration forever. Here are some general rules:

- Bands that have had their songs in an Apple ad are still marginally acceptable.
- Bands that have had their songs in ads for other companies are not acceptable.
- If you mention a band you like and the other person has heard of it, you lose. They own you. It is essential that you like the most obscure music possible.

Remember, popular artists can turn unpopular in a heartbeat (Ryan Adams, Bright Eyes, the Strokes), so you would be best to stick to the following statements: "I love Arcade Fire"; "I still think the Montreal scene is the best in the world"; "I would die without Stereogum or Fluxblog"*; and "Joanna Newsom is maybe the most original artist today."

---

*Never replace Stereogum with Pitchfork, which is one of those things that used to be cool but is now not cool.

What Are White People Listening To?

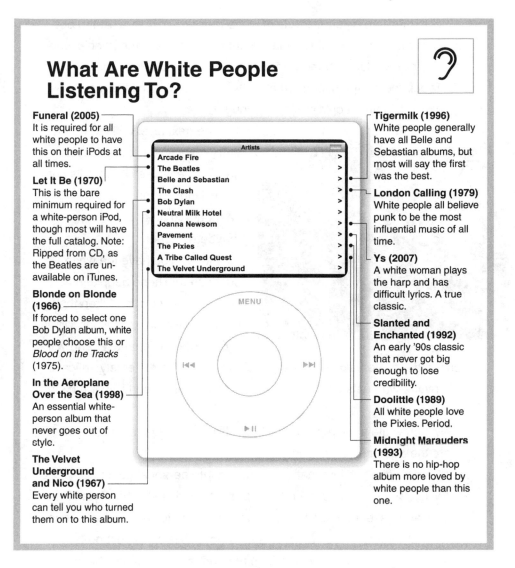

Funeral (2005)
It is required for all white people to have this on their iPods at all times.

Let It Be (1970)
This is the bare minimum required for a white-person iPod, though most will have the full catalog. Note: Ripped from CD, as the Beatles are unavailable on iTunes.

Blonde on Blonde (1966)
If forced to select one Bob Dylan album, white people choose this or *Blood on the Tracks* (1975).

In the Aeroplane Over the Sea (1998)
An essential white-person album that never goes out of style.

The Velvet Underground and Nico (1967)
Every white person can tell you who turned them on to this album.

Tigermilk (1996)
White people generally have all Belle and Sebastian albums, but most will say the first was the best.

London Calling (1979)
White people all believe punk to be the most influential music of all time.

Ys (2007)
A white woman plays the harp and has difficult lyrics. A true classic.

Slanted and Enchanted (1992)
An early '90s classic that never got big enough to lose credibility.

Doolittle (1989)
All white people love the Pixies. Period.

Midnight Marauders (1993)
There is no hip-hop album more loved by white people than this one.

Artists

- Arcade Fire
- The Beatles
- Belle and Sebastian
- The Clash
- Bob Dylan
- Neutral Milk Hotel
- Joanna Newsom
- Pavement
- The Pixies
- A Tribe Called Quest
- The Velvet Underground

MENU

42 | Sushi

Regardless of whether they are vegetarian, vegan, or just guilty about eating meat, all white people love sushi. To them, it's everything they want: foreign culture, expensive, healthy, and hated by the "uneducated."

But there are different levels of white-person sushi love. At the bottom are the spicy tuna/California roll eaters. These are the people who get their fix at places named Rock And Roll!, Magic Sushi Company, or Trader Joe's–type supermarkets. Often this sushi isn't the most authentic, but white people can't get enough!

The next level up is the entry-level sushi snob. These are people who still love rolls but are willing to branch out to salmon and tuna sashimi, maybe even eel.

Finally, you have the white sushi snob. These people just take it all way too far. Often they will sit only at the sushi bar, will try to order in Japanese, and will only order the *omakase.* These people will often be extremely critical of anyone who eats a roll of any type or does not properly flip the nigiri into his mouth.

When white people get sushi, they all want to order sake to complete the authentic experience.

So how can this information be turned into personal gain?

White people are obsessed with finding good sushi; therefore, if you offer to take them to "the best sushi place" in town, you are sure to have them accept. If you are an Asian man, this is an almost no-fail method of getting dates with white girls, and maybe, just maybe, joining Bruce Lee and Paul Kariya's dad.

In addition, going out for sushi is considered a special evening in white-person culture. Not as special as brunch, but still, it comes with expectations.

But what if the person you are interested in is a vegetarian? Not a problem. For some reason, most white people who say they are vegetarians will eat sushi. Apparently, fish aren't cute enough to warrant inclusion with pigs, chickens, and cows.

Plays

While white people certainly love "the cinema," they are required to balance their interest in film with an interest in live theater, most notably, plays.

In spite of plays having minimal sets, no special effects, an intermission, and a higher admission price, white people believe that live theater is essential to any cultured city. It is not known if white people actually enjoy plays or if they are just victims of massive peer pressure from the 75 percent of white people who have acted in a play at some point in their life.

The only real advice around this subject is to never accept an invitation from a white person to go see a play. Often you will be supporting their friend or cousin and then get stuck with a $45 ticket (at least) and three hours of trying to figure how close you are to the end.

Public Radio

The lack of a television has left many white people without viable entertainment, and as much as they would like to believe that they can read books during every moment of their free time, it's simply not possible. They need something to fill the gap and provide background noise while they play on the Internet. They need public radio.

Public radio provides white people with news and information that has the proper perspective (their own). It is very important for white people to have a news source that isn't tied to profits or major corporations; public radio has the freedom to pursue hard-hitting stories and provide the only truly objective voice in the national media. Because if a news outlet were to depend on one source for their funding, it would

have to constantly produce stories that interest and reassure that group, thus making it almost worthless to people outside of that group. You are probably thinking, "Wait a second, doesn't public radio get most of its money through donations by white people?" If so, you are right, and while this sort of explains NPR's programming choices, political bias, and staff, it's not a good idea to point it out to white people.

But not everything is political. Public radio also features *This American Life,* hosted by Ira Glass. For white women without a television, he is considered the ideal man (ahead of Jon Stewart). The program features a collection of white people doing stories about minorities and the wrong kind of white people. It is very entertaining and is the safest and easiest way for white people to learn about these groups.

There are many other shows, and literally anything you hear is an appropriate and excellent topic of conversation, provided you announce that you heard about it on NPR before approaching the subject. For example: "I heard this fascinating piece on NPR about chlamydia. It got me thinking, do any of you have an STD?" Normally this would be a very offensive question, but phrased in the context of NPR it is considered acceptable.

Overall, the lesson here is that if you want your time with white people to go smoothly, there are few things you can do that are more effective than listening to public radio.

Asian Fusion Food

In much the same way white people often believe that adding truffle oil to something will always make it better, there is a long-standing belief that adding "Asian" to anything is an improvement. The most popular things for white people to infuse with "Asian influence" are furniture, film, animation, interior design, personal style, children, and perhaps most important, food.

It is true that many white people demand especially authentic Asian food and will often seek out the most authentic experiences. However, these restaurants generally do not feature staff who understand the question "Yes, but did you use these same pots to cook any meat? You see, I'm vegan, and I cannot eat any vegetables that were prepared in pots that have been used to cook meat."

An Asian fusion restaurant is a fantastic compromise where white people can use chopsticks and get definitive answers about the use of gluten in the food, all while being surrounded by modern black furniture and Asian-inspired art.

With their beautiful wait staff, décor, and trendy music, these restaurants are the equivalent of a white guy with an Asian girlfriend and a Chinese or Japanese character tattoo that says "truth."

The bar at an Asian fusion restaurant will also feature a full list of drinks that are made with exotic Asian liquors like soju. White people cannot resist the opportunity to prove to their friends that they are not only wine experts, but true connoisseurs of sake. If you need to gain their trust, ask for a recommended drink—they will love it.

Because of their high cost and small portions, these locations are best used for formal dinners. As such, if a white person invites you to one, it can be appropriately interpreted as a romantic gesture.

46 | The Sunday New York Times

Mornings are exceptionally important to white people, as witnessed by their love of brunch places. However, some white people never go out for breakfast on a Sunday morning. The reason? The Sunday edition of *The New York Times.*

A perfect white Sunday generally works like this: Wake up at around 8:45; if the paper has been delivered, retrieve the paper and begin a pot of coffee. If the paper has not been delivered, a white person will go out and usually buy the supplies needed for breakfast—bagels, orange juice, lox, cream cheese, or waffle mix. Some white people even pick up freshly brewed coffee with the paper!

Once coffee, food, and the newspaper have been procured, white people put on extra-mellow music (jazz, classical, or, for the cooler ones, ambient trip-hop or something along those lines). They then proceed to read each section of the paper, stopping periodically to tell their partner about the interesting news they have just seen. "Looks like another civil war might break out in Africa"; "Did you see that the Met is doing *Tristan and Isolde*?"

White couples usually fight over who gets to read the Sunday *Magazine* first. How do we know this? They will tell us repeatedly about how they always fight over the Sunday *Magazine.*

But note well that the sports section will always remain perfectly creased and unread, unless they have a teenage son. So on Monday morning, if you need to impress your co-workers, choose to talk about something you read in the *Book Review,* the *Magazine,* or Sunday Styles.

All white people are expected to read the Sunday *Times.* You are given an exemption during your early college years, but by age 22 it is pretty much law.

 # Liberal Arts Degrees

When white people go to college, they tend to study what are known as the Liberal Arts. This includes actual Art, English, History, Classics, and Philosophy. These can, of course, be broken down further into Film, Womyn's Studies (yes, the spelling is correct), Communications, Gender Studies, and so forth. It is important to note that a high percentage of white people also get degrees in Political Science, which is pretty much like Liberal Arts, and only seems to have the word *science* in it to make white people feel better about themselves.

These degrees enable white people to spend four years of their lives reading books, writing papers, and feeling great about themselves. It is a known fact that Liberal Arts students firmly believe that they are doing you/society a favor by reading Proust and not getting a job. They then protest for reduced tuition, more money for the arts, and special reduced student rates on things like bus passes.

But what about the white people who study Science, Engineering, and Business? Unless they become doctors, they essentially lose white-person status (which can be regained only by working at a nonprofit).

So why would white people spend all that time studying and work-ing to get into college if they are just going to read books that they

Literary	Artistic	Film	Gourmet
Journalism student	Art history major	Film student	Study abroad in France
↓	↓	↓	↓
Copywriter	Art teacher	Production assistant	Waiter
↓	↓	↓	↓
Journalist	Gallery assistant	Film festival coordinator	Chef
↓	↓	↓	↓
Editor	Graphic designer	Alternative newspaper film critic	Vegetarian caterer
↓	↓	↓	↓
Writer	Artist/ photographer	Director	Organic restaurant owner

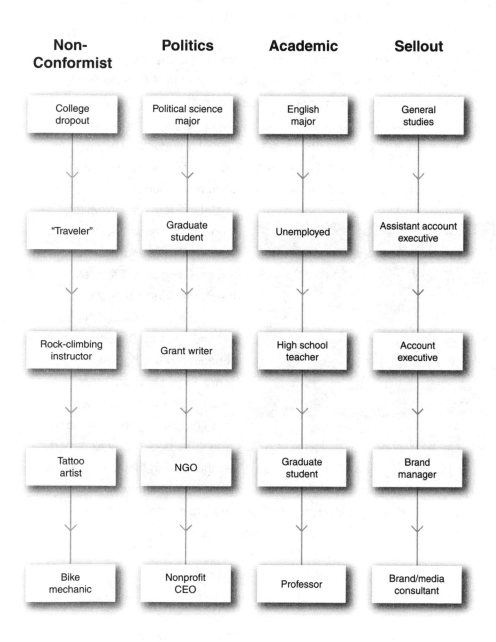

Non-Conformist	Politics	Academic	Sellout
College dropout	Political science major	English major	General studies
"Traveler"	Graduate student	Unemployed	Assistant account executive
Rock-climbing instructor	Grant writer	High school teacher	Account executive
Tattoo artist	NGO	Graduate student	Brand manager
Bike mechanic	Nonprofit CEO	Professor	Brand/media consultant

White
Career Trajectories

might have read in their free time? Because white people have it made. They can take that degree and easily parlay it into a job at a nonprofit, in an art gallery, or in publishing. If the pay is low, no problem—their parents will happily help out with rent until they magically start making six figures or nonmagically turn 40.

White people can also take that degree and go to graduate school, and eventually become professors or adjunct professors. They will still require parental support. If they are *really* ambitious and need to make money, they can take that degree and go to law school.

But the real reason white people need these degrees is so that they can sound smart at parties. Of course, it trickles down to making connections, getting hired, knowing rich people, and so forth. But ultimately it all begins by saying, "Reading Henry James was the most rewarding part of undergrad."

Using this to your advantage can be very difficult as attempts to talk about the books they skimmed while hungover can mate them hate you for exposing them. It is best to say that you were a first-generation college student and your parents demanded that you study math, chemistry, economics, or computer science. You had to read Joyce on your own.

48 Whole Foods and Grocery Co-ops

White people need organic food to survive, and where they purchase this food is as important as what they buy. In the community, Whole Foods stores have replaced churches and cathedrals as the most important and relevant buildings in society. There are some regions that do not have Whole Foods but do have an abundance of white people (college towns). In these situations Whole Foods can be substituted with a local co-op grocery store.

All of these stores are pretty much the same: lots of vegetables, grain-fed free-range meat and eggs, and soy everything. They are also characterized by an outrageously large section of vitamins, supplements, and natural oils. There are natural, handmade soaps that give these stores a distinct identical smell.

Many white people consider shopping at Whole Foods to be a religious experience, one that allows them to feel good about their consumption, with the use of paper bags and biodegradable packaging. The numerous pamphlets outlining the company's policy on hormones, genetically modified food, and energy savings belie the fact that Whole Foods is a profit-driven, publicly traded corporation that has wisely discovered that making white people feel good about buying stuff is outrageously profitable.

As you walk through a Whole Foods or co-op you will see white people pushing carts, buying things like flaxseed oil, wine, tofu versions of meat, and organic kohlrabi. These stores also provide prepared foods, which single white people often purchase to avoid cooking. This is important information, as this section of the store is loaded with single white people.

These stores are excellent places for taking children, as there is nothing that they actually want.

"Oh, Mommy, look, chocolate!"

"No, Joshua, that's carob."

"I want it."

"OK."

The child will then take a bite and realize that nothing in the store can be trusted.

 # Vintage

The love affair between white people and old stuff goes back literally hundreds of years. In the older days it was almost exclusively contained within the realm of furniture. However, while white people still love antiques, these don't always fit so well with a modern lifestyle and kitchen.

Beginning in their late teens, white people begin an obsession with finding cool vintage clothing at local thrift shops and Goodwill stores. Making purchases at these locations helps to meet a number of white-person needs.

First, it allows them to say, "Oh, this? I got this shirt at Goodwill for three dollars." This statement focuses the attention on the shirt, taking attention away from the $350 jeans and $200 shoes. The white person can then retain that precious "indie" cred.

Second, it allows a white person to have something that other white people don't. This is an important consideration when trying to determine the worth and ranking of white people.

As white people get older, and the opportunities to wear a "Pittsburgh Special Olympics '76" T-shirt diminish, they must move their vintage fetish from clothes to furniture and knickknacks. Often the only thing that a post-30 white person can hang on to is furniture. The mention of a "vintage stove" or "vintage card catalog" can send their imagination racing about how to incorporate it into their current home decor. By having at least one unique vintage piece of furniture in a room full of IKEA, white people can still tell themselves that they are unique and cooler than their friends.

When you enter a white person's home, you should immediately search for anything not made by IKEA, Crate & Barrel, or Anthropologie. Upon finding such an item, you should ask, "Where did you get that? It's really cool." The white person will then tell you a story about how they acquired it, allowing them to feel cool and reminding them that they have fantastic taste.

50 Irony

White people hate a lot of stuff (Republicans, TV, Vin Diesel movies, SUVs, fast food), but every once in a while they turn that hate into sweet irony.

White people will often make a joke about how hard it is to define irony. It's not that funny, and back in the '90s people got all upset at Alanis Morissette for using the term improperly in her song "Isn't It Ironic?" But the reason that white people love irony is that it lets them have some fun and feel better about themselves.

The most horrific recent example is trucker hats, which shockingly went from mainstream in the '80s to ironic in the early 2000s and then almost immediately back to mainstream. So now the hats are not rare or unique in any way. Once something reaches this stage, irony cannot be restored for a decade.

Other examples would include white people getting together to have a "white trash" night, where they will eat Kentucky Fried Chicken, drink Bud Light, and watch Larry the Cable Guy or *The Marine,* or maybe listen to Kid Rock or P.O.D. These events allow white people to

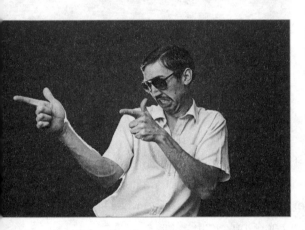

experience things they are supposed to hate, all while feeling better about their own lives, decisions, and cultured tastes.

Occasionally, white people will put an ironic knickknack in their home or apartment such as a "Support Our Troops" magnet or a bottle of Mickey's.

This can be used to your advantage. If you need to appear cool to white people, you just need to pick something that was popular ten-plus years ago and put it in a prominent place at your desk or in your home. A C+C Music Factory cassette and a "2 Legit 2 Quit" T-shirt would be good examples.

Also, you might find yourself in a conversation where you mention that you like something, and there is an awkward silence indicating that it is not cool. In this situation, you must say, "Oh yeah, I also like [insert similar things in such a way to show that you were kidding about that first thing]" and smile. The white people will laugh and all will be well.

51 Living by the Water

It is hardly a secret that all white people love being near water. And why wouldn't they? It provides so many of the activities that they love—swimming, kayaking, canoeing, sailing—and it's a perfect place to read.

Before we move on, let's not gloss over that last point. White people love to be near a body of water so they can read a book while sitting nearby. The process of reading is somehow heightened through the process of doing it near water. Extreme reading!

When you think long-term, it's important to realize that all white people own/wish to own/plan to own/will own some sort of property near a body of water. Rather than say all white people want to live on the ocean, it's important to break it down across the regions.

On the West Coast, all white people want to live as close to the beach as possible. One look at the demographics for Manhattan Beach, Santa Monica, Hermosa Beach, Newport Beach, and Laguna Beach will reveal this fact through tangible numbers.

On the East Coast, many white people dream of owning oceanfront property in New England, where they can make their lives as close as possible to a J. Crew catalog.

And in the landlocked states, the dream of lakefront property is alive and well.

White people will often purchase second homes near water if they cannot accommodate the dream in their own city. Usually they want it to be within driving distance, but the need for life near water is so great that they will even consider buying in other countries.

To white people, a view of water from the house is their greatest achievement in life. And you should remember this when discussing your hopes and dreams with them. It is also important that you choose a water sport (swimming, fishing, kayaking, etc.) that you pretend to like. That way, you can talk about how, when you move to your waterfront property, you can just wake up in the morning and [insert water-based activity], right out of your front door.

Mountain views are also acceptable, but are generally seen as a poor substitute.

Sarah Silverman

White people love to laugh, so it's no surprise that some of the funniest people in the world are white! But do not believe that white people find all types of humor funny. BET Comic View, for example, is not considered funny and white people generally get little to no enjoyment out of the program.

The easiest way to find out if comedians are approved by white people is to see if they get mentioned on music blogs or have ever given an interview in which they talked about how much they love the Magnetic Fields, Of Montreal, or the Shins. But this does not guarantee white-person acceptance.

If the topic of comedy comes up, the best thing to do is talk about how much you love Sarah Silverman. White people can't get enough of her! Her whole shtick is saying really offensive things! But it's OK, because she's pretty and has a small voice, so it all sounds so cute! Get it? It's not offensive, because she says racist or sexist things that she knows are offensive. So it's OK.

Much as white women will say that Jon Stewart is their perfect man, it is fully acceptable and encouraged for white men to say that Sarah Silverman is their perfect woman.

Sarah Silverman is also considered an "alternative comic," which essentially means she is universally loved by white people, but not enough to be a movie star.

Other acceptable "alternative" comedians: David Cross and the Comedians of Comedy (Patton Oswalt, Brian Posehn, Zach Galifianakis, and Maria Bamford). Also, white people will say they love any comedian who shares your ethnicity. For example, if you are Korean, watch how many times white people tell you how much they like Margaret Cho.

WARNING: Under no circumstances should you *ever* list Dane Cook as your favorite comedian. The wrong kind of white people like him. And mentioning him will cause white people to lose all respect for you.

Dogs

A lot of cultures love dogs, be they for entertainment, labor, or food. But white people love dogs on an entirely different level.

It should be understood that in white culture, dogs are considered training for having children. All white couples must get a dog before having kids. This will prepare them for responsibility by having another creature to feed, love, and toilet train. Because of this, white people generally assume that their dog is their favorite child unless otherwise stated.

When actual children are born, the dog is not displaced but rather remains as the most important member of the household. This is because of the fact that white children will eventually hate their parents, but dogs will love anyone who feeds them.

White people generally believe that dogs have human emotions and that they are capable of loving certain TV shows, films, and music. "Buster just loves watching *Six Feet Under*!"—even though most dogs

would enjoy watching Hitler if they got attention every time he was on TV. They also believe that their dogs share similar tastes in food—"Little Ben Kweller likes the organic food the best"—forgetting the fact that dogs enjoy eating their own feces, as well as pretty much anything that falls onto the floor.

When searching for homes, many white people will require large yards so that their "dog can run around." If you work in real estate, this can be exploited for large markups when selling to white people.

It is also a proven fact that dogs are often used by white people to attract members of the opposite sex. Bringing a puppy or dog to a local dog park will encourage interaction and conversation. Even more so than a Mac laptop.

If white people talk about their dogs it is essential you reassure them that their dogs are absolutely special and unique. Furiously agree that treating dogs like children is the only way to care for a pet. Under no circumstances should you *ever* say anything that is derogatory toward dogs, critical of spoiling dogs, or implies that dogs are not full members of society who deserve the same rights as humans. Doing any of these three things will completely destroy your relationships.

54 | Kitchen Gadgets

White people are under a lot of pressure to enjoy cooking. Everything in their culture tells them that they need to have nice kitchens and that they need to cook with organic, fresh ingredients to make delicious, complicated food. Though

any great chef can prepare fantastic meals with a knife and a few pots, white people believe they need a full cadre of appliances and gadgets in their kitchens in order to live up to expectations.

If you go into a white person's kitchen you will find a waffle maker, a rice cooker, a steamer, a food processor, a panini press, and a blender. There will also be hand-powered devices like flour sifters, ravioli crimpers, pizza cutters, potato ricers, and a sushi mat.

But in order to truly enter into whitedom they need to own the holy grail of white kitchens—the KitchenAid stand mixer. They will match this mixer to their kitchen's color scheme and it will make up the focal point. And much like many religious artifacts, it will remain untouched for months and even years, sitting on the counter to be admired as a testament to their lifestyle.

Kitchen gadgets also serve as one of the main reasons why white people get married. Look at their registry and you will find products for any possible kitchen task. If you end up buying one of these for a white person, your card should mention the beautiful food that you hope you can eat together one day. This kind of stuff goes over like gangbusters.

If you find yourself locked in a conversation about kitchen gadgets, a good way to say a little but mean a lot is to mention, "I find the consumer models to be poorly built, but my friend, a chef, brings me with him to a restaurant supply shop that's not open to the public. The stuff there is high quality. It's where I get all my pans."

If this is too big a risk, you should just throw out a combination of these terms: Le Creuset, Calphalon, All-Clad, Williams Sonoma, and Sur le Table. White people go so nuts when they hear these words. You won't even have to finish your sentence.

Apologies

White people know that their ancestors did some messed-up things. As a result, it has become hard-wired for them to apologize for almost anything.

In fact, white people are so used to apologizing that they start all sentences that might cause disagreement with "I'm sorry." For exam-

ple, "I'm sorry, but *Garden State* was a better film than *Hard Eight.*" In other cases, white people will apologize without being asked.

"Excuse me, Dylan. You dropped a piece of paper in front of my desk."

"Oh, sorry about that!"

It's just that easy! Just point it out and they'll apologize.

Sometimes if you are out late at night and a white person irritates someone at a nightclub or a bar, the first thing they will do is apologize in rapid-fire mode in hopes it will stop them from getting their ass kicked. This technique has a surprisingly high success rate, as the aggressor immediately knows that fighting this person will be very easy and provide little satisfaction.

Lawyers

To understand why so many white people become lawyers, it is essential to understand the story and conflict behind every decision to enter law school.

When white people reach the final year of their arts degree they are faced with a horrible realization: their degree is worthless. This realization is especially harsh since most white people have spent the previous three years assuming that they would be immediately offered a six-figure job as a travel writer or film executive upon graduation. They  soon realize that there are thousands of other white people moving to San Francisco and New York searching for work in publishing, other media, and the nonprofit sector.

As if this wasn't enough of an insult, white people also learn that the salaries in these fields are not enough to support a white lifestyle. Organic food, trips to India, Priuses, microbrews, modern furniture, and condominiums are all very expensive and very essential to white people.

Without a trust fund, many white people are forced to figure out how they can somehow take their lemon of a degree and turn it into highly profitable lemonade. It does not take very long before they realize that law school is the answer to all their problems.

By attending law school, white people are able to make six figures without having to do math. They can also spend three more years in school and eventually move to a city of their choosing, where they will be greeted with a job and a standing invitation to drink with colleagues at a bar.

The latter is especially important, since TV and film have created a common white fantasy of being a lawyer, working late, then meeting friends at a bar where men have loosened their ties and women have opened a few buttons on their shirts. After drinking, they return home to a loft or modern condo, where they pour another drink before falling asleep.

Of course, this fantasy and career path only describes white people who are looking for respect, profit, and upward social mobility. They are regarded as some of the top people in white culture, but they can be trumped. If you are talking to a group of white people who are in or are planning to go to law school, it is important that you say, "I'm going to law school but I don't want to be a lawyer."

Not only does this prove that they are smart enough to go to law school, but it shows that they are motivated by more than just the crass pursuit of money. If you can follow it up by saying you plan to use your degree to help artists or poor people, you win.

57 Documentaries

It is a confirmed fact that white people make up the overwhelming majority of both documentary film makers *and* viewers. They just can't get enough!

Within white culture the words "documentary filmmaker" are code for "unemployed." With few deadlines and virtually no budget pressures, documentary filmmakers are able to spend upwards of eight years working on a film. When a white person lists this as their profession, you should never ask when the film is coming out, as it's considered poor taste to put pressure on them.

As viewers, white people like to watch these films because it helps them to get a basic grasp on a complex issue in an hour or two.

After watching a political documentary, white people often feel as though they have learned enough to begin teaching others about what they saw in the film. Perhaps you noticed the increase in health-care policy scholars in 2007, or American foreign-policy experts in 2004, or gun-control pundits in 2002.

These are all references to white hero Michael Moore, the film-maker who has produced a body of work responsible for reaffirming things that white people already believe in. Generally, white people get very excited about documentaries that will confirm they are right. Sadly, Moore's ability to actually change the way people think has been marginal.

Sometimes white people will watch a documentary to learn about a new subject; these are called "foreign documentaries" and are an important part of white discourse. In fact, they are second only to celebrity endorsement in terms of creating white passion around a subject.

Be aware that an invitation to see a documentary film will often involve watching the film, suffering through a question-and-answer period, and potentially ending up with the filmmaker sleeping on your couch.

 # Japan

Though there is full white consensus on a number of white things, there is perhaps nothing that draws more universal white acclaim than the island nation of Japan. It should be noted that some white people harbor *some* ill will toward Japan because of whaling, killing dolphins, or the Rape of Nanking, but those are generally considered isolated incidents that do not indict the entire nation.

White people love Japan for a number of reasons. Sushi is pretty much the biggest one, since white people have spent so much time in sushi restaurants enjoying the food, learning how to eat it, and most important, how to be snobby about it. This natural curiosity fills them with a need to pay a visit to Tsukiji and taste the freshest sushi possible.

But it goes beyond food. All white people either have taught/will teach/ wished they had taught English in Japan. It is a dream for them to go overseas and actually live in Japan. This helps them not only because it fills their need to travel, but it also enables them to gain important leverage over other white people at sushi restaurants when they can say, "This place is pretty good, but living in Japan really spoiled me. I've had such a hard time finding a really authentic place."

White people also love Japan because of its tradition, futuristic cities, films, kawaii stuff, music, and writers. Many white nerds are into anime, so being too into this can be seen as a negative by white people. It's best to have a passing familiarity with things like Hayao Miyazaki, who is universally accepted by white people. If they don't know who he is, they will look him up and they won't find weird violent or sexual cartoons.

If you find yourself in the midst of an awkward silence when talking to white people, just mention that you want to go to Japan. They will immediately begin talking about their trip to Japan, or their favorite stuff from Japan, but it will be entirely about them. This is useful as you no longer have to talk, and they will like you for letting them talk about themselves.

As with anime, you have to be careful about how much you like

Japan. If you know how to speak Japanese you kind of ruin it for everyone else.

Natural Medicine

One thing all white people believe is that natural medicine can cure everything. If you want to test this theory, think about which stores supply the bulk of natural/herbal remedies. That's right! Whole Foods and organic co-ops!

Because of its rather shady history, white people do not trust the pharmaceutical industry. Using pretty sound logic, they believe that the drug companies have no motivation to find real cures for things like

AIDS, since the real profits are in drugs like Viagra and Xanax. With their powers of deduction, white people have determined that herbal remedies are unilaterally better than anything produced by a drug company.

Since white people can't really blame any race for their problems, they need to blame corporations. In this case, the

reason that they are sick or fat or without energy is because the drug companies are in a conspiracy to keep them addicted to placebos. This helps them shed accountability and lets them feel like they are helping the environment by rejecting the polluting, greedy, awful drug companies and taking natural, organic medicine from the Earth.

But perhaps it goes deeper. Hundreds of years ago, another group of people believed firmly in natural medicine and its ability to cure disease. Then white people gave them blankets with smallpox, and they all died. So perhaps turning to natural medicine also helps white people feel better about killing natives.

How can you use this for gain? It's easy! When white people you work with are feeling sick or say they have no energy, ask them to tell you more about their problems. After pretending to listen for a little while, tell them that in your culture/home country, "We cured that using a special herbal powder from [insert made-up tree] root."

Then the next day take them a small bag of basil or oregano and tell them to boil it in a tea (white people love to believe in magic teas) and see how they feel in the morning. One of two things will happen. They will either wake up feeling great because they want to feel great and they'll thank you profusely, or they will wake up feeling like crap, and when you confront them at work, they will lie and say they feel good.

Either way, you did them a favor, so now they owe you a favor.

Note: It's weird that there are some white people who won't take aspirin but will take Ecstasy, cocaine, Xanax, and Vicodin.

Toyota Prius

Over the years, white people have gone through a number of official cars. In the '80s it was the Saab and the Volvo. By the '90s it was a Volkswagen Jetta or a Subaru 4WD station wagon. But these days there is only one car for white people; one car that defines all that they love: the Toyota Prius.

The Prius might be the most perfect white product ever. It's expensive, gives the idea that you are helping the environment, and requires no commitment or life changes other than having slightly less money.

The Toyota Prius gets 45 miles per gallon. That's right, you can drive 45 miles and burn only one gallon of gasoline. So somehow, through marketing or perception, the Prius lets people think that driving their car is *good* for the environment. It's a pretty sweet deal for white people. You can buy a car, continue to drive to work and to Barack Obama rallies, and still feel like you are helping the environment!

Some white people pull the ultimate move: Prius, Apple sticker on the back, iPod rocking, and Democratic candidate bumper sticker. Unstoppable!

There are a few ways you can use this to your advantage. If you are carpooling to an event or party you can always say, "Can we take your Prius? My car doesn't get good mileage and I feel guilty driving it." And bam! Free ride!

Also, if you see a white person in a Prius you can say, "Wow, it's great to see that you're doing something for the Earth." The white person will feel very good about themself and offer to drive you home or to IKEA, or to drop you off at '80s night.

Bicycles

A good place to find white people on a Saturday is at a bike shop. Bike shops are almost entirely staffed and patronized by white people!

But not all white people love bicycles in the same way. There is much diversity. First up, we have the younger urban white folks who absolutely love their fixed-gear bicycles. These are seen all over college towns, Silverlake in L.A., Williamsburg in Brooklyn, Queen West in Toronto, and Victoria, British Columbia. Fixed-gear bicycles meet a lot of requirements for white-person acceptance. They can be made from older (i.e., vintage) bicycles, thus allowing the rider to have a unique bike that is unlikely to be ridden by anyone else in town. They are also easily customizable with expensive things: Aerospoke rims, Phil Wood hubs, and Nitto parts. The combination of rare bicycles and expensive parts makes it easy for white people to judge other white people on the quality and originality of their bicycles. This is important in determining if someone is or isn't cooler than you.

Some white people also like mountain bikes because they let them be in nature. It really isn't any more complicated than that.

And finally, many white people love expensive road bikes and the accompanying Spandex uniforms. These enable them to ride long distances and to wear really tight clothes without any social stigma. This type of rider will spend upward of $5,000 on a bicycle and up to $400 on accessories but will not ride to work—perhaps because they cannot wear the Spandex there. It is important that you never question why someone needs a $5,000 bicycle, since the answer is always "performance."

For the most part, these rules are unisex. But there is a special category of bicycle that appeals far more to white women: the European city bike (pictured). White women have a lot of fantasies about idealized lives, and one of them is living in Europe and riding around an old city on one of these bikes. They dream about waking up and riding to a little café, visiting bakeries and cheese shops, and finally riding home to prepare a fancy meal for their friends, who will all eat under a canopy decorated with white Christmas lights. This information can be used to help gain the trust/admiration of a white woman, especially if you can pull off a lie about how your mother used to do all these things when she was younger.

And of course, it goes without saying that white people who ride bikes like to talk about how they are saving the Earth. If you know a person who rides to work, you should take them aside and say, "Hey, thanks. Sincerely, the Earth." Then give a thumbs-up. That white person will ride home on a cloud.

62 | Knowing What's Best for Poor People

White people spend a lot of time worrying about poor people. It takes up a pretty significant portion of their day. They feel guilty and sad that poor people shop at Wal-Mart instead of Whole Foods, that they vote Republican instead of Democratic, that they go to community college or get a job instead of studying art at college.

It is a poorly kept secret that, deep down, white people believe that if given money and education, all poor people would be *exactly* like them. In fact, the only reason that poor people make the choices they do is because they have not been given the means to make the right choices and care about the right things.

A great way to make white people feel good is to tell them about situations where poor people changed how they were doing things because they were

given the "whiter" option. "Back in my old town, people used to shop at Wal-Mart, and then this nonprofit organization came in and set up a special farmer's co-op so that we could buy more local produce, and within two weeks the Wal-Mart shut down and we elected our first Democratic representative in forty years." White people will first ask which nonprofit, and are they hiring? They will be so filled with euphoria that they will invite you to more parties so you can tell this story to their friends.

WARNING: It is *essential* that you make it clear that poor people do not make decisions based on free will. To suggest anything to the contrary could crush white people and their hope for the future.

Expensive Sandwiches

Having already covered breakfast and dinner options, the question remains: What do white people like to do for lunch? The answer: eat expensive sandwiches.

If you need to find a cache of white people, get yourself to a sandwich shop. Generally these places aren't open for dinner, have a

panini press, and are famous for their bread. There are always vegan options and the selection of meats and cheese is mostly from Europe.

The waiters and waitresses in these places are highly coveted by the white population. They are not quite as cool as bartenders, not quite as snobby as coffeeshop workers, but still artsy, young, and more than likely to be a musician/artist/writer (since they only have to work from 11:00 to 3:00).

If you are in the position where you need to take a white person to lunch for business or pleasure, saying "I know a great sandwich shop" will always bring out a smile. The white person will then tell you about the great sandwich shop in the town where they went to college and how they had a crush on a waiter, or that there was a special sandwich they always ordered. This will put the person in a good mood.

It's important to note that this type of restaurant is best for business or friendship situations, as it is very neutral and does not carry romantic connotations as sushi and breakfast do. So if a white person that you are interested in decides to invite you for a sandwich, do not assume it will lead to any sort of sexual conduct.

These sandwiches generally start at $8.99. Remember that whenever a white person says they want to go to a sandwich shop you are looking at at least a $15 outlay after tip and drink, $20 if the place has a good selection of microbrews.

Also note: White people will wait up to 40 minutes for a good sandwich.

 Recycling

Recycling is part of a larger theme of stuff white people like: saving the Earth without having to do that much.

Recycling is fantastic! You can still buy all the stuff you like (bottled water, beer, wine, organic iced tea, and cans of all varieties), and then when you're done you just put it in a *different* bin from your other garbage. And boom! Environment saved! Everyone feels great. It's so easy!

This is important because all white people feel guilty about producing waste. It doesn't stop them from doing it, of course. Deep down they believe they should be like the Native Americans and use every part of the product or beast they have consumed. For many white people this simply means putting plastic bags into a special drawer, where they will accumulate until they are eventually used to carry gym clothes or a bathing suit. Ultimately this drawer will get full and will be emptied only when the person moves to a new home. Advanced recyclers use them as garbage bags.

If you are in a situation where a white person produces an empty bottle, watch their actions. They will first say, "Where's the recycling?" If you say, "We don't recycle," prepare for some awkwardness. They will make a move to throw the bottle away, hesitate, and then ultimately throw the bottle away. But after they return, look in their eyes. All they can see is the bottle lasting forever in a landfill, trapping small animals. It will eat at them for days, so at this point you should say, "I'm just kidding, the recycling is under the sink. Can you fish out that bottle?" And they will do it 100 percent of the time!

The best advice is that if you plan to deal with white people on a regular basis, either start recycling or purchase a large blue bin so that they can believe you do it.

 # Coed Sports

White people love being outside, but they don't often have time for marathons or ten-mile bike rides. The answer is to play coed sports. This provides white people with a valuable opportunity to make friends with other white people and maybe even find a date.

Many white people play in their first coed league in college. It is considered good form to talk about how you played in one of these leagues, when the best player on your team was a girl. This will make everyone feel better and remind them of the benefits of supporting women's athletics.

As white people move into careers, the coed leagues become important tools for bonding with co-workers and making valuable career connections. Popular coed sports include kickball, softball, flag foot-

ball, and soccer. Although kickball used to be kind of cool, it's sort of played out. So unless it's work-related, it's not really worth joining a kickball league any-more.

On the surface, these events seem like friendly contests, with everyone having a laugh. But danger lurks, and within them exists the possibility to ruin your reputation and hard-earned status with white people. It is key that you properly match your athletic ability to your surroundings.

If you are a poor athlete, rest easy. Coed sports were made for you! But if you are reasonably skilled in sports, you have to be extremely careful how you approach your coed matches. If you try *too* hard (bowling over a female catcher, throwing a kickball *extra* hard at someone), you come off as an aggressive, crazy maniac. On the other hand, if you don't try at all, you come off as a jerk who thinks they are above the game. The only solution is to approach it like a point-shaving basket-ball player—play hard enough to be convincing, but not hard enough to win.

If you follow these rules, you will find yourself invited to the manda-tory postgame drinks at a local bar, where you will be photographed many times.

Divorce

If you are in a room with more than five white people it is a statistical certainty that at least two of them have divorced parents and at least one has an ex-wife or husband. The divorce rate among white people is sky-high, and it is one of the most easily exploited aspects of white culture.

The combination of alcohol and stories about divorce is the easiest and most efficient way to gain the trust and admiration of a white person. If your parents never divorced and you are required to lie, do not worry about being called out. White people spend most of their day waiting for opportunities to complain about their parents, and they will likely only ask questions about your scenario to be polite. Say whatever you like, they are only waiting for trigger expressions to enable them to return to their own story. Popular ones include *unhappy, work, affair, tough time at school,* and *tied down.* Say any of these and the white person will immediately redirect the conversation back to their situation.

When the night finally ends, you will be operating on a friendship level that normally takes eight to ten months.

If the white person is actually going through a divorce, do not be too concerned. A lifetime of difficult breakups has prepared them for the event. They are well equipped to become the center of attention for their friends and family. The best thing you can do in this scenario is to constantly reassure the white person that they deserve better. It will comfort them instantly. This is due to the fact that all white people believe they deserve more than they have. Hearing it from someone else helps to confirm the injustice of fate and gives them hope that they will eventually receive the sexual and career payday that is long overdue.

Finally, if you have a deceased parent do not bring it up when white people are talking about divorce. You will immediately be crowned the winner of the pain party, but you will also make all the white people feel bad for making such a big deal out of nonfatal divorce.

Standing Still at Concerts

Music is very important to white people. It truly is the soundtrack to their lives, meaning that white people are constantly thinking about what songs would be on the soundtrack of their biopic. The problem is that most of the music white people like isn't especially dance-friendly. More often the songs are about pain, love, breaking up with someone, not being able to date someone, or death.

So when white people go to concerts at smaller venues, what do they do? They stand still! This is an important part of white concertgoing, as it enables you to focus on the music, and it will prevent drawing excess attention to yourself. Remember, at a concert everyone is watching you, just waiting for you to try to start dancing. Then they will make fun of you.

The result is Belle and Sebastian concerts, which essentially look more like a disorganized line of people than musical events.

If you find yourself invited to a concert with a white person, do *not* expect to dance. Prepare yourself for three hours of standing reasonably still. It is also advised to get a beer or (if legal) a cigarette so you have something to do with your hands, although it is acceptable to occasionally raise one hand and point just above the stage.

Note: The addition of the drug Ecstasy changes everything.

Michel Gondry

When compiling the canon of directors that white people like, one must include Michel Gondry. He has directed such white classics as *Eternal Sunshine of the Spotless Mind, The Science of Sleep,* and *Dave Chappelle's Block Party.* Oh, that's right, Charlie Kaufman, Gael García Bernal, *and* Dave Chappelle—could it get any better for white people? Oh yes, it could.

You see, Michel Gondry got famous by directing videos for the White Stripes, Massive Attack, and Björk. These are three acts that, at some point in their lives, all white people have thought were cool.

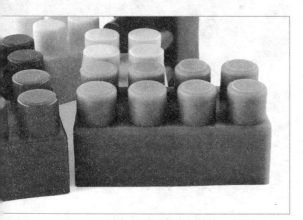

Between the ages of 16 and 20, all white people go through a phase in which they aspire to become a music-video director. This is followed shortly by a phase in which they want to become a regular director. In both cases, they don't want to produce generic content, they want to create art. As a result, the two directors who have achieved this (Spike Jonze is the other) are universally beloved by white people.

If you look at the DVD collection of a white person (even one without a TV), you will find *The Work of Director Michel Gondry.*

This knowledge can be used to help find common ground with white people. Talk about how you wanted to direct music videos after you saw Michel Gondry's video for "Around the World" by Daft Punk.

Then make a joke about how foolish you were at that age, and everyone will have a good laugh. But they will also feel your pain about sacrificing your artistic dreams.

Mos Def

In the olden days of white culture, people used to look up to kings and princes. These were the people they adored, and every night they wished and hoped that somehow they could wake up and be just like them. But with royal families crumbling, that role has been filled by one man: Mos Def.

He is everything that white people dream about: authentic ("He's from Brooklyn!"), funny ("He was on Chappelle's show!"), artistic ("Have you heard 'Black on Both Sides'?"), an actor ("He's in the new Gondry film!"), and not white ("I don't see race"). He has done an amazing job of being in big-budget movies (*The Italian Job*) and having one of his songs ("Ms. Fat Booty") become a white-person wedding staple but still retaining authenticity and credibility.

If you find yourself in a social situation where you are asked to list your favorite actor or artist, you should always say Mos Def. That way you can name someone that everyone has heard of and you don't look like you are trying to one-up anybody. The only possible negative consequence is some white people might think, "I wish I had said that first."

70 Difficult Breakups

Prior to engaging in divorce, most white people train for it by engaging in a series of long-term relationships that end very poorly. At some point you will likely encounter a white person who is in the middle of a difficult breakup with a boyfriend or girlfriend.

The suffering of heartbreak is universal, but it is important to be aware that white people thrive during these trying times. If you play your cards right, you can parlay these moments into future favors and valuable trust.

The majority of white-person art is created after a difficult breakup; films, indie music, and poetry are all kicked into high production during the end of a relationship. This helps white people prepare for the pain that is coming.

Once breakup proceedings have been initiated, a white person immediately becomes the center of attention in their circle of friends. During this time they are permitted to talk at great length about themselves, listen to the Smiths, and get free dinners from friends who think, "They shouldn't be alone right now."

It is imperative that you do not attempt to kick them out of their misery by saying things like "Get over it," "There are other people out there," or "I don't want to read your poem." Implying that there are things in the world more important to you than their breakup is considered one of the rudest actions possible.

If you are lucky enough to speak a second language, the best thing you can do for a white person in this situation is to give them an expression in that language that relates to breaking up. This will make them feel better since they are comforted by the gesture and happy to be learning a new expression that they can repeat to their friends.

71 Being the Only White Person Around

This concept ties heavily into #7, Diversity, and #19, International Travel, but it is important that you fully understand how white people view authenticity and experience.

In most situations, white people are very comforted by seeing their own kind. However, when they are eating at a new ethnic restaurant or traveling to a foreign nation, nothing spoils their fun more than seeing another white person.

Many white people will look into the window of an ethnic restaurant to see if there are other white people inside. It is determined to be an acceptable restaurant if the white people in there are accompanied by ethnic friends, but if there is a table occupied entirely by white people it is deemed unacceptable. The arrival of the "other white people" at either restaurants or vacation spots instantly means that lines will grow, authenticity will be lost, and the euphoria of being a cultural pioneer will be over.

Being aware of this can be extremely valuable in your efforts to gain the trust of white friends and co-workers. If you take a white person to an ethnic restaurant and another white person (or group of white people) shows up, you can lose all respect and trust that you have worked so hard to acquire. Do your best to find a table with a divider, or ask the waiter to put future white people out of sight.

Note: This does not apply to nightclubs.

72 | Study Abroad

In addition to accumulating sexual partners, binge drinking, drug use, and learning, white people consider studying abroad to be one of the most important parts of a well-rounded college education.

Study abroad allows people to leave their current educational institution and spend a semester or a year in Europe or Australia. Though study abroad is offered to other places, these are the overwhelming favorites.

By attending school in another country, white people are technically living in another country. This is important, as it gives them the

opportunity to insert that fact into any sentence they please. "When I used to live in [insert country], I would always ride the train to school. The people I'd see were inspiring."

If you need to make up your own study-abroad experience, they all pretty much work the same way. You arrived in Australia not knowing anybody, you went out to the bar the first night and made a lot of friends, you had a short relationship with someone from a foreign country, you didn't learn anything, and you acquired a taste for something (local food, beer, fruit). This latter point is important because you will need to be able to tell everyone how it is regrettably unavailable back home.

It is also important that you understand the study-abroad ranking system. Europe/Australia form the base level, then Asia, then South America, and finally the trump card, studying abroad in Tibet. Then there is the conversation killer of studying abroad—Africa. If you studied in Africa, it is usually a good idea to keep it quiet; it will remind white people that they were too scared to go and they will feel bad. Use this only in emergencies.

73 | Gentrification

In general, white people love situations where they can't lose. While this is already true for most of their lives, perhaps the safest bet a white person can make is to buy a house in an up-and-coming neighborhood.

White people like to live in these neighborhoods because they get credibility and respect from other white people for living in a more "authentic" neighborhood where they are exposed to "true culture" every day. So whenever their friends mention their homes in the suburbs or wealthier urban areas, these people can say, "Oh, it's so boring out there, so fake. In our neighborhood, things are just more real." This superiority is important as white people jockey for position in their circle of friends. They are like modern-day Lewises and Clarks, except that instead of searching for the ocean, they are searching for old houses to renovate.

In a few years, if more white people start moving in, these initial trailblazers will sell their property for triple what they paid and move into an ultramodern home. Credibility or money; either way, they can't lose!

When one of these white people tells you where they live, you should say, "Whoa, it's pretty rough down there. I don't think I could live there." This will make them feel even better about their credibility and status as neighborhood pioneers.

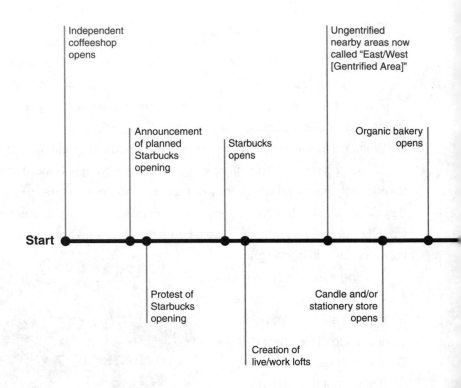

Start

Independent coffeeshop opens

Announcement of planned Starbucks opening

Starbucks opens

Ungentrified nearby areas now called "East/West [Gentrified Area]"

Organic bakery opens

Protest of Starbucks opening

Candle and/or stationery store opens

Creation of live/work lofts

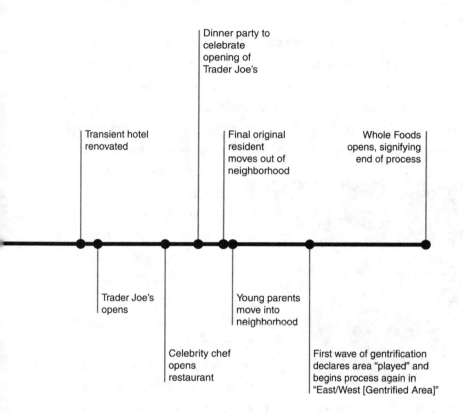

Dinner party to
celebrate
opening of
Trader Joe's

Transient hotel
renovated

Final original
resident
moves out of
neighborhood

Whole Foods
opens, signifying
end of process

Trader Joe's
opens

Young parents
move into
neighborhood

Celebrity chef
opens
restaurant

First wave of gentrification
declares area "played" and
begins process again in
"East/West [Gentrified Area]"

Gentrification
Timeline

74 Oscar Parties

One of the best places to gain a white person's trust is at an Oscar party. An invitation to one of these parties is your "foot in the door."

It is absolutely essential that you prepare in advance for the party. As you should know by now, white parties are never just about "showing up and having fun." They require planning, preparation, and (in the case of the best parties) costume preparation. The first step for succeeding at an Oscar party is to get your language in order. You should *never* say "movie," always say "film." You should also familiarize your-

self with which categories use the term "Best" and which use "Outstanding Achievement in." Saying something like "I hope *Atonement* wins Best Art Direction" is a good way to guarantee you won't be invited next year.

We briefly touched on the importance of costumes, which can take a good white party and make it great. Oscar parties are no exception, and if you are invited to a party with a dress code, it is imperative that you arrive in costume or you'll make everyone else feel like a jerk.

Choosing a costume is fairly simple. It is always best to dress as a character from a nominated film. So for the 2008 Oscar party it might be best to put a pillow under your shirt and come as a pregnant teenager in tribute to *Juno* (but by no means should anyone bring an actual pregnant teenager). Dressing up as a character from a previous Oscar-winning film is also acceptable but seen as slightly less fun.

Though it may not have been stated on the invitation, white people love to apply their party theme to the entire event, including food. Even if they have no plans for themed food, you cannot lose by bringing something that ties into the ceremony. Again using *Juno* as an example, if you were to come to the party with jugs of SunnyD, it would highlight your keen observation of detail when it comes to watching films. Then the white people will see that you watch films the same way they do. Also be prepared to be involved in an Oscar pool, but make sure you don't win. If you do, just say that you were lucky.

However, all of this preparation will mean nothing if you do not act correctly during the most important part of the night: when the nominees are read for Best Foreign Film. At this point someone will get angry and state that some movie that no one has heard of was snubbed. When this happens just nod and agree. Mention that it sounds interesting and that you will watch it tomorrow, even if you have already seen it and know that it's boring.

Basically what separates Oscar night from other party nights is that it allows white people to express themselves through their tastes in film. If they see that you are someone who agrees with a majority of their opinions, then they will be your friends and provide you with ample opportunities to sip wine and attend film festivals together.

75 Threatening to Move to Canada

White people often get frustrated with the state of their country. They do not like the president, or Congress, or the health-care system, or the illegal status of marijuana. Whenever they are presented with a situation that seems unreasonable to them, their first instinct is to threaten to move to Canada.

For example, if you are watching TV with white people and there is a piece on the news that they do not agree with, they are likely to declare, "OK, that's it, I'm moving to Canada."

Though they will never actually move to Canada, the act of declaring that they are willing to undertake the journey is very symbolic in white culture. It shows that their dedication to their lifestyle and beliefs is so strong that they would consider packing up their entire lives and

moving to a country that is only slightly different from the one they live in now. Within white culture, it is agreed upon that if Canada had better weather it would be a perfect place.

Be aware that this information can be used quite easily to gain the trust of white people. Whenever they say, "I'm moving to Canada," you must immedi-

ately respond with "I have relatives in Canada." They will then expect you to tell them about how Canada has a perfect health-care system, legalized everything, and no crime. Though not true, it will reassure them that they are making the right choice by saying they want to move there. But be warned, they will refer to you in future conversations and possibly call on you to settle disputes about Canadian tax rates. So use this advice only if you plan to do some basic research.

Note: Canadian white people threaten to move to Europe.

Note: Europeans are unable to threaten to move anywhere.

76 | Bottles of Water

Water seems like a fairly simple concept. You turn on the tap, put a glass underneath, and drink. Sadly, it is not that simple for white people. On the whole, they are unable to put a glass under a tap and just drink. In fact, this is such a strange concept that the City of New York had to launch a rather large PR campaign to show white people that it was actually possible to drink the water that comes out of the tap!

Up until that point, white people were consuming most of their water in the form of expensive bottles of Fiji or Evian. To this day, many white people continue to get their water in this fashion, and it is important to be aware about how your choice of water can say a lot about who you are.

Logically, you would assume that drinking the most expensive premium bottled water (Fiji and Voss) would be enough to show the world that you are too good for tap water. And a few years ago you would have been right. But lately, advanced white people have been getting very upset about all the waste that comes with drinking 15 to 20 bottles per week.

Nowadays more advanced white people have started to use sturdier, refillable bottles. But do not assume this is from the tap. Most white people need to run their water through some sort of filter (Brita or PUR) before they put it into their bottles. This allows them to feel good about using a refillable bottle, but it also makes it more complicated, which they also like.

Previously, the gold standard was the Nalgene bottle, but recent studies have shown that the plastic can leak toxins into the water. Currently, white people on the cutting edge are really into metal bottles of water with twist caps. It is recommended that you buy one of these as soon as possible. Having one will give you precious leverage over any white person who is drinking from a plastic bottle. "Oh, bottled water? Really? I mean, it's cool, but I kind of thought you cared about the Earth." If you see someone drinking a Fiji water you have the opportunity to go in for the kill. "Do you know that your bottle of water has a bigger carbon footprint than me? I think they were originally going to call it Aboriginal Blood but that bottle was as close as they could get. You know, legally."

Again, this should only be used in extreme situations.

Following your confrontation, the white person is likely to have a metal bottle just like yours. If this happens, there will be an implicit pact whereby they will do favors for you provided you do not tell everyone they got their bottle after seeing yours.

Musical Comedy

One of the more interesting things about white people is that they love singing comedians.

This style of humor involves a person or group singing a song, but instead of being serious, the song has funny lyrics. It's not any more complicated than that, yet white people can't get enough of it. Weird Al Yankovic, Tenacious D, Sarah Silverman (sometimes), Flight of the Conchords, Dennis Leary, and Adam Sandler are all excellent examples of the genre.

It's a pretty good idea, because when you have jokes that aren't that great and music that isn't that great, you can just mix them together to create something that will entertain white people.

So how can you use this knowledge to your advantage? If you find yourself at a corporate retreat where you have to put on a skit for the other employees in your office, it's always a good idea to suggest doing a funny song. The rest of your group will get very excited and start work immediately on some clever lyrics. Do not worry about the music part. If you have more than two white males on your team, it is certain that one of them can play the guitar.

78 Multilingual Children

All white people want their children to speak another language. There are no exceptions. They dream about the children drifting between French and English as they bustle about the kitchen while they, as parents, read *The New York Times* and listen to jazz.

As white people age, they start to feel more and more angry with their parents for raising them in a monolingual home. At some point in their lives most white people attempt to learn a second language and are generally unable to get past ordering in a restaurant or overpronouncing a few key words. This failure is not attributed to their lack of effort, of course, but rather their parents, who didn't teach them a new language during their formative years.

White people believe that if they had been given French language instruction when they were younger, their lives would have turned out very differently. Instead of living in the United States, they would be living and working abroad for the United Nations or some other organization with headquarters in Switzerland or The Hague.

Generally, white people prefer their children to speak French. Advanced white people will actually spend outrageous amounts of money to send their children to a Lycée or Ecole Française. But the vast majority will abandon their dreams when they realize that they will someday need a second mortgage so their child can one day have a better study-abroad experience in France.

Languages such as German, Spanish, Swedish, or Italian are also acceptable, but are considered to be poor substitutes, especially

Spanish. At the time of writing, it is considered expert-level white-person behavior to have the children speaking Asian or African languages.

There is only one way to use this information to your advantage: speaking another language means that white people are more likely to want to have children with you. It is seen as a cheaper alternative to language schools.

Modern Furniture

When white people envision their dream home, a key part of the fantasy involves at least one piece of furniture designed by a famous architect from the '30s.

Architects like Mies van der Rohe and Le Corbusier designed iconic modern furniture that has inspired virtually everything made by

IKEA and Design Within Reach, both of which are key suppliers of furniture to white people. As with all things, white people will do whatever it takes to secure authenticity, including paying thousands of dollars for a small piece of furniture. If they are able to acquire this prized furniture, they will forever refer to it only by the designer's name. "I spend hours in the van der Rohe, just looking through these beautiful books of his work."

Referring to a white person's expensive chair as a "chair" is considered poor form and will likely result in a loss of trust and/or respect. The best strategy for avoiding this faux pas is to look for the most uncomfortable chair in a white person's home and ask,

"Who designed that?" If they say "IKEA" or "Design Within Reach," you can call it a chair; otherwise refer to it only by the name they give you.

It should also be noted that many white people are unable to acquire this furniture, but that does not mean you cannot use this information to your advantage. In situations where you need to improve your connection with a white person, just mention how you hope to be successful enough to one day afford an original piece of furniture by (insert obscurely named architect). If they have heard of the designer they will nod in agreement; if they have not, they will also nod in agreement and make a note to look it up later.

In either case, your status will rise.

 # The Idea of Soccer

Many white people will tell you that they are very into soccer. But be careful. It's a trap.

If you then attempt to engage them about your favorite soccer team or talk about famous moments in soccer history, you are likely to be met with blank stares. This is because white people don't actually enjoy watching soccer. They just like telling their friends that they are into it.

In fact, the main reason white people like soccer is so they can buy a new scarf. As you may or may not know, many soccer teams issue special scarves, and white people cannot get enough of them!

Most white people choose a favorite soccer team based on either a study-abroad experience or a particularly long vacation to Europe or South America. When they return, they like to tell their friends about how great "football" is and that they are committed to "getting more into it" now that they have returned home. Some white people take this charade so far as to actually play in adult soccer leagues or attend local professional matches.

The best method for exploiting this tendency is to ask a white person who their favorite football team is and how they came to be a fan. This will allow them to tell you about their time abroad and feel as though they have impressed you with their knowledge. Once they have finished talking, it is acceptable to ask for favors.

Note: European white people actually are into soccer and are exempt from this entry. However, they are free to use it to their advantage when in North America.

Graduate School

Being white means to engage in a day-in, day-out struggle to prove that you are smarter than other white people. By the time they reach college, most white people are confronted with the fact that they may not be as smart as they imagined.

In coffeeshops, bars, and classes white people will engage in conversations about authors and theorists that go nowhere as both parties start rattling off progressively more obscure people until eventually one side recognizes one and claims a victory. By the time they graduate (or a year or two afterward), white people realize that they will need an edge to succeed in the cutthroat world of modern white society.

That edge is graduate school.

Though professional graduate subjects like Law and Medicine are desirable, the true ivory tower of academia is most coveted, as it imparts true, useless knowledge. The best subjects are English, History,

Art History, Film, Gender Studies, [insert nationality] Studies, Classics, Philosophy, Political Science, [insert European nationality] Literature, and the ultimate: Comp. Lit. MFAs are also acceptable.

Returning to school is an opportunity to join an elite group of people who have a passion for learning that is so great they are willing to forgo low-five-figure publishing and media jobs to follow their dreams of academic glory.

Being in graduate school satisfies many white requirements for happiness. They can believe they are helping the world, complain that the government/university doesn't support them enough, claim they are poor, feel as though they are getting smarter, act superior to other people, enjoy perpetual three-day weekends, and sleep in every day of the week!

After acquiring a master's degree that will not increase their salary or hiring desirability, many white people will move on to a PhD program, where they will attempt to realize their dream of becoming a professor. However, by their second year they usually wake up with a hangover and realize: "I'm going to spend six years in graduate school to make $35,000 a year and live in the middle of nowhere?"

After this crisis, a white person will follow one of two paths. The first involves dropping out and moving to New York, San Francisco, or their original hometown, where they can resume the job that they left to attend graduate school. At this point, they can feel superior to everyone still in graduate school and say things like "A PhD is a testament to perseverance, not intelligence." They can also impress their friends at parties by referencing Jacques Lacan or Slavoj Zizek in a conversation about *American Idol.*

The second path involves becoming a professor, moving to a small town, and telling the local residents how they are awful and uncultured.

It is important to understand that a graduate degree does not make someone smart, so do not feel intimidated. They may have read more, but in no way does that make them smarter, more competent, or more likable than you. The best thing you can do is to act impressed when a white person talks about critical theorists. This helps them reaffirm that what they learned in graduate school was important and that they are smarter than you. This makes white people easier to deal with when you get promoted ahead of them.

82 Hating Corporations

One of the more popular white-person activities of the past fifteen years has been attempting to educate others on the evils of multinational corporations. White people love nothing more than explaining to you how Wal-Mart, McDonald's, Microsoft, or Halliburton is destroying the Earth's cultures and resources.

While the growth of multinational corporations can be attributed to

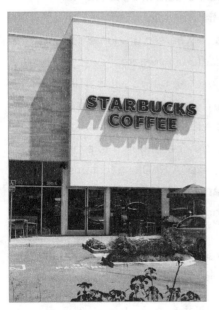

a number of complex social, economic, and political factors, many white people prefer to take the word of two trusted sources: *No Logo* and *AdBusters.*

No Logo, published in 2000, has been responsible for more white-person "enlightenment" than any book since the burning of the library at Alexandria. By reading this one magic book, white people are able to get a full grasp on the evils of multinational corporations and then regurgitate them to friends and family.

Advanced white people will supplement *No Logo* with a subscription to

AdBusters, where they will learn how to subvert corporate culture and return it to the masses. Specifically, this means taking ads and redoing them to create a negative message about a product. Apparently the belief is that when other people see this ad, they will be hit with an epiphany that their entire existence has been a *Matrix*-style manufactured universe.

If you plan to engage in lengthy conversations or get high with white people it is recommended that you read *No Logo* or an issue of *AdBusters.* Failing that, it is acceptable to buy a copy to leave on your coffee table. When white people see it, they will recognize you as someone who can see through the advertising and has a proper perspective on life.

WARNING: When engaging in a conversation about corporate evils it is important to *never, ever* mention Apple computers, Target, or IKEA in the same breath as the companies mentioned earlier. White people prefer to hate corporations that don't make stuff they like.

83 | Bad Memories of High School

The most time- and cost-efficient way of gaining a white person's trust and friendship is to talk to them about their high-school experience.

Virtually every white person you meet was a nerd in high school—that's how they were able to get into a good arts program or law school. As such, their memories of high school are painful but not tragic, since they were able to eventually find success in the real world. Exploiting this information is your one-way ticket into the heart of a white person.

Your first priority must be to steer the conversation to the topic of high school, which is not very difficult. If you are talking about music, mention the music you think they would have liked in high school and how you were taunted for liking those bands. If you cannot properly gauge the type of music a white person liked in high school, you should always say that you were really into the Cure. All white people know that liking the Cure in high school is an invitation to be tortured by the cool kids. This will bring about instant sympathy and respect.

It is also acceptable to discuss how you were in love with a cool kid who never loved you back. For added effect, you can mention how said cool kid is now doing very poorly and that you are excited for the upcoming reunion.

If these first two points are not enough to gain an adequate level of trust, you can close the deal by saying, "I was the only [insert ethnicity] kid in Improv/on the paper/on the student council." Wait for a sympathetic look and then you will know that you have forged an unbreakable and easily exploited bond.

For maximum effectiveness, this technique should be used in a social group setting where everyone can share their stories. By guiding the conversation, you will be seen as a natural and sympathetic leader. This can be easily exploited for professional and social gain.

Note: In the rare event that you meet a white person who was "cool" in high school, do not panic. There is a 100 percent chance that one of their other cool friends sold them out in a coup for control of their social circle. They will tell you all about it. Failing that, you can exploit the inherent guilt they feel about their treatment of nerds.

T-shirts

Many people and cultures view T-shirts as simple pieces of apparel that can be acquired cheaply and worn in casual situations. For white people, they are never that easy. The T-shirt is one of the most complex and expressive items in their entire wardrobe.

Your choice of casual wear says a lot about you. There are stringent rules and hierarchies associated with T-shirts that you must know before venturing into any white-dominated social situations.

T-shirts fall into three categories: vintage, new, and unacceptable, with the latter category comprising the bulk of the world's supply. Within each category lies another, more precise subset of rules and rankings. This is complicated, make no mistake.

The most prized T-shirt category is vintage. As shown earlier, white people need authenticity like they need oxygen, and ownership of an original vintage T-shirt from the '70s or '80s is a very powerful social status symbol. The ideal shirt will have a funny logo, a year attached to it, and will be as thin as rice paper. In the event that two white people have shirts that meet these criteria, the superior ranking is given to the person who paid the least for the shirt. Acquiring a shirt at a vintage clothing store is seen as less respectable than sorting through racks at Goodwill.

The second category of T-shirt is new, and there really are only two options. The first is American Apparel, a company that constantly reminds you it is based in downtown Los Angeles. It is considered an acceptable white company since it produces things that are very simple but also very expensive. The second acceptable new shirt is Thread-less. This Chicago-based company produces artistic and funny T-shirts that are acceptable for concerts, trips to Whole Foods, and '80s night. White people like these shirts so much because they are designed by white people for white people. Sort of like a white FUBU.

Finally, and perhaps the most important to be aware of, is the un-acceptable category of T-shirt. There are a few simple rules to follow in order to avoid wearing the wrong one. First, if it's made of a stiff, thick cotton, throw it in the garbage immediately. White-people T-shirts must be made of the softest, finest organic cotton. This is law. Unless it is vintage, the shirt cannot be made in a foreign country (unless you can certify its labor conditions). The shirt cannot contain a current sports logo. Shirts with sports logos are acceptable, but they must contain a logo that hasn't been used in 15 years. Last and not least, it cannot be baggy. Your T-shirt must be tight-fitting for both style and mating pur-poses.

It is also imperative to understand that faux vintage shirts ("Getting Lucky in Kentucky") are completely unacceptable. They are beloved by the wrong kind of white people, and must be avoided at all costs.

This information is best applied when you are planning on attend-ing a social gathering. Your T-shirt says a lot about you, and if it's the right kind of shirt it will set white people at ease. Also, asking a white person, "Where did you get that shirt?" will allow them to tell you a de-tailed story about how they acquired it. This will enable them to assert the reason their shirt has a higher ranking than yours.

85 | *The Wire*

Though white people have a natural aversion to TV, there are some exceptions. For white people to like a TV show it helps if it is critically acclaimed, low-rated, shown on pre-mium cable, and/or available as a DVD box set.

The latter is important so that white people can order it from Netflix and tell their friends, "I'm really into [insert series] and I watched ten episodes in a row this weekend. I'm almost caught up."

If you attempt to talk about an episode they have not seen yet, they will scream and cover their ears. In white culture, giving away information about a film or TV series is considered as rude as spitting on your mother's grave. It is an unforgivable offense. Recent series that have fallen into this category include *The Sopranos, Six Feet Under,* and most recently *The Wire.*

For the past three years, whenever you say *"The Wire,"* white people are required to respond by saying "It's the best show on television." Try it the next time you see a white person! Though now they might say "It *was* the best show on television."

So why do they love it so much? It all comes down to authenticity. A long time ago, someone started a rumor that when *The Wire* is on TV, actual police wires go quiet because all the dealers are watching the show. Though this is not true, it seems plausible enough to white people and has imbued the show with the needed authenticity to be deemed acceptable.

The popularity of this show among white people has created a unique opportunity for personal gain. If you need to impress a white person, tell them you are from Baltimore. They will immediately ask you about *The Wire* and how accurate it is. You should confirm that it is "like a documentary of the streets." The  white person will then slowly shake their head and say "Man" or "Wow." You will be seen in an entirely new light.

If you are not from Baltimore but the white person you are talking to is, they might start asking you a lot of questions. In this situation, you should just say you left when you were young but you still have a lot of cousins there but you don't like to go back to visit. This will remove all doubts and they can go back to telling you about how John from Accounting needs to "stop snitching" about their two-hour lunch breaks.

Shorts

One thing prized by white people is making the most of situations. They like to maximize opportunities for all that they are worth. This applies to jobs, vacations, investments, books, education, and perhaps most important, warm days.

After a prolonged cold snap, white people are very excited at the

first hint of a warm day. It is their opportunity to go back outside, to enjoy nature and thrive. In order to get the most enjoyment possible out of these days, white people turn to one of their most trusted allies: shorts.

It is a known fact that white people believe they can cause spring to arrive early by wearing a pair of shorts on any day that is slightly above seasonal temperatures. This myth runs so deep that they will often wear shorts the following day when temperatures drop, at which point they will refuse to admit that it is cold.

When you encounter a cold white person in shorts it's best to say, "I can't wait until it's warm enough to go windsurfing." They will likely give you a high five.

87 | Outdoor Performance Clothes

As white people get older, they like to have clear boundaries between their professional and personal lives. They don't mind talking about their personal life at work, but they hate talking about their work life when they are enjoying a weekend or vacation.

But with BlackBerrys and laptops, white people could be working anywhere, at any time. So how do you know when they are off the clock? It's easy: just check their clothes.

When white people aren't working, they generally like to wear outdoor performance clothes. The top suppliers of these garments and accessories include North Face, REI, Mountain Equipment Co-Op, Columbia Sportswear, and Patagonia. When you see white people wearing these brands, it is important that you do not discuss business matters. Instead you should say things like "Where did you get that fleece?" and "What's that thing holding your keys to your shorts?" White people will be more than happy to talk to you about their sustainably produced possessions.

The main reason white people like these clothes is that they allow them to believe that at any moment they could find themselves with a Thule rack on top of their car headed to a national park. It could be 4:00 P.M. on a Saturday when they might get the call: "Hey, man, you know what we need to do? Kayak then camping, right now. I'm on my way to get you. There is no time to change clothes."

Though it is unlikely that they will ever receive this call, white people hate the idea of missing an opportunity to enjoy outdoor activities just because they weren't wearing the right clothes.

If you plan on spending part of your weekend with a white person, it is strongly recommended that you purchase a jacket or some sort of "high-performance" T-shirt, which is like a regular shirt, just a lot more expensive.

88   Having Gay Friends

If white people could draft friends the way that the NFL drafts prospects it would go like this: black friends, gay friends, and then all other minorities would be drafted based on need and rarity in the region.

When choosing gay friends, white people like to base their decision on their own needs and requirements. Younger white people tend to prefer young, social gay people. This is their all-important ticket into nightclubs and parties.

When straight people go to a gay nightclub, they are reminded of how progressive and tolerant they are. If they are hit on by a member of the same sex, it provides them with a valuable story that they can use to prove to their other friends that they are more progressive and tolerant. "This guy/girl hit on me, I said I was 'straight but not narrow,' and it was totally chill. Oh, you went to an Irish bar this weekend? That's cool, I guess."

Older white people prefer to be friends with gay parents because it enables their children to experience much-needed diversity with people who are, for all intents and purposes, exactly the same as them.

It is also worth noting that a gay friendship of any sort allows white people to feel as though they are a part of the gay rights movement. While white people love being a part of any movement, the gay movement is especially important to them because they can blend in at rallies and protests and spend an afternoon feeling the sting of oppression.

Gay friends are an essential part of a white person's all-star diversity roster. But white people are always on the lookout for the ultimate friend: a gay minority. Above all, it is generally accepted that a gay black friend with a child is considered a once-in-a-lifetime opportunity—like a quarterback who can pass, run, kick, and play linebacker. White people will crawl over each other for the opportunity to claim this person as a friend and add them to their roster of diversity.

Once a white person has told you about their gay friends, it is recommended that you say "I wish more people were like you" every few months. This will allow them to feel good about their progressive choice of friends and remind them that they are better than other white people.

If you follow this simple rule, you should be able to maximize all benefits of white friendship, including moving help and free drinks.

 St. Patrick's Day

Normally if someone wakes up at 7:00 A.M., takes the day off work, and gets drunk at a bar before 10:00 A.M., they are an alcoholic, and not in the artistic, edgy way that white people are so fond of.

On March 17, however, this exact same activity is called celebrating St. Patrick's Day. This very special white holiday recognizes St. Patrick, the patron saint of Ireland, who helped to bring Catholicism to the Emerald Isle. His ascetic life is celebrated every year by white people drinking large amounts of Irish-themed alcohol and listening to the Dropkick Murphys.

It is also the day of the year when you can make the greatest gains in your social and professional relationships with white people.

Most of the time, white people consider celebrations of European heritage to be racist unless they ignore large swathes of the sixteenth through twentieth centuries. But since the Irish never engaged in colonialism and were actually oppressed, it is considered acceptable to celebrate their ancestry—even encouraged. For this reason, 100 percent of white people are proud to claim that they are somewhat Irish.

A big part of St. Patrick's Day is having white people feel particularly upset at the oppression of their ancestors, which has in no way trickled down to them. If you find yourself talking with a white person who tells you about how their great grandfather was oppressed by both the English and the Americans, it is strongly recommended that you lend a sympathetic ear and shake your head in disbelief. It is never considered acceptable to say, "But you're white now, so what's the problem?"

It is also worth noting that on this day there is always one trump card that never fails to gain respect and acclaim. When you are sitting at an Irish bar and someone orders a round of Guinness, you must take a single sip, and while the other white people are savoring their drink, you say, "Mmmm, I know it sounds cliché, but it really is true: Guinness just tastes better in Ireland."

This comment will elicit an immediate and powerful response of people agreeing with your valuable insight. This statement also has the additional benefit of humiliating the members of your party who have not been to Ireland (and thus cannot confirm this proclamation). Having not traveled to Ireland and consumed a beer that is widely available in their hometown and throughout the world, they will immediately be perceived as provincial, uncultured, and inferior to you.

It is also strongly encouraged that you memorize the lyrics to "Jump Around." They will come in handy.

90 Dinner Parties

Though many would have you believe that white people come of age at summer camp, it's simply not the truth. Immediately following graduation but prior to renovating a house, white people take their first step from childhood to maturity by hosting a successful dinner party.

It is imperative that white people know how to host a good dinner party, as they will be expected to do it well into retirement.

At the most basic level, these simple gatherings involve three to six couples getting together at a single house or apartment, having dinner, and talking for five to six hours. Though it might seem basic, dinner parties are some of the most stressful events in all of white culture.

Hosts are expected to deliver a magical evening. The food must be homemade with fresh, organic ingredients, the music must be just right (edgy, new, but not too loud), and the decor of the house should be subtle but elegant. The ultimate goal is to do a better job than the couple who hosted the last dinner party while attempting to make everyone jealous and sort of dislike you.

The dinner party is the opportunity for white people to be judged on their taste in food, wine, furniture, art, interior design, music, and books. Outside of dictatorships and a few murder trials, there might not be a more rigorous judgment process in the modern world. Everything must be perfect. One copy of *US Weekly,* a McDonald's wrapper, a book by John Grisham, a Third Eye Blind CD, or an *Old School* DVD can undo months and maybe even years of work.

Even before guests arrive, the pressure on the host is immense, and it does not let up once dinner begins. While eating, drinking, and conversation are expected to fill up five or six hours, sometimes it's just not enough. In order to fill the silence, white people will often turn to board games (Cranium!) or Wii Bowling. This lets everyone have fun together without having to really talk to each other.

It is strongly encouraged to bring a gift to these dinner parties, usually either wine or some kind of dessert. If you are able to bring a particularly rare dish from your culture, you will be the star of the party. To seal the deal, be sure to explain as much as you possibly can about the dish: history, availability, and the proper way to eat it. Every white person at the party will be taking mental notes and will be in your debt for introducing them to something new and authentic. If a white person says they have eaten the dish before, it is best to respond by saying, "You ate a watered-down version. They don't even sell this to white people, it's that intense. Even I had to show ID."

The entire party will universally acknowledge you as the top guest. Even the hosts will appreciate you for bringing diversity to the table in the form of both food and person.

Autobiography: A White Life

Instructions: In a dinner party setting, photocopy these pages and distribute them to your guests. Have each person fill in the blanks with accurate answers from his or her life. Have each person score themselves using the guide provided, then discuss. Reward the whitest person at the party with a trendy pastry from an organic bakery.

Scoring: +1 point for all accurate answers. Bonus points awarded as indicated.

Autobiography by _____. (+5 for two last names)
FULL NAME

I was born in a suburb of _____. I hated every
CITY

second of it. Growing up, I just wanted to be so much more, and I

knew I would be a famous _____ in
RESPECTED CREATIVE CAREER

_____ (+2 for international city). Middle school was
BIGGER CITY

pretty uneventful, except I remember trying _____
SUBSTANCE

(+2 for drugs) for the first time and getting really sick. I should have

learned my lesson then, but of course I didn't.

I was so unbelievably awkward in high school, it was terrible.

I didn't make things any easier by being a part of

the_____ (-1 for sports team). We were such nerds. I was
EXTRACURRICULAR ACTIVITY

always so jealous of the cool kids and their parties, and secretly

I always hoped I would get invited to one. Then, one time in my

_____ year I actually got invited! I was so excited
FR/SO/JR/SR

_____ was going to be there. I was so ob-
OBJECT OF CRUSH

sessed with _____. When I got there, _____ didn't even
HIM/HER   HE/SHE

notice that I was alive.

That year, all I did was fantasize about leaving. I got into

_____ (+3 for liberal arts college, +2 for Ivy, +1 for state school) and could
COLLEGE OR UNIVERSITY

not wait to get there and completely reinvent myself. My first

year was incredible: I took all of these great classes in

_____ and _____ (+1 for each liberal arts discipline,
SUBJECT   SUBJECT

-1 for science, -1 for math, -2 for business). Eventually I would switch my major

_____ (+1 for twice, +2 for three times, +5 for four or more) times before settling
NUMBER

on _____ (+1 for liberal arts, -1 for science, -1 for math, -2 for business).
MAJOR

I played _____ (+5 for Ultimate Frisbee, +4 for rugby, +4 for lacrosse, +2 for
SPORT

kickball, +1 for softball) in college and had a great time. After our games

we used to go to this great local _____ shop and I
<small>FOOD</small>

would always order the _____. Too bad I can't find a
<small>MENU ITEM</small>

good one in this city!

I will never forget the time that I saw _____ <small>(+10 if music</small>
<small>MUSICIAN OR BAND</small>

<small>eventually factored in Apple commercial)</small>. It was before they got big. It was in-

credible—so intimate.

By the time I reached the end of my sophomore year, I had ex-

perimented with _____ <small>(+1 for drugs, +3 for bisexuality, +1 for student</small>
<small>REGRETTABLE EXPERIENCE</small>

<small>government)</small>, and I made up my mind to never do it again unless

presented with an exceptional opportunity. Around the same

time, I had to make up my mind about where to do my study

abroad. It was a tough choice between _____ and
<small>CONTINENT</small>

_____, but ultimately I settled on _____
<small>CONTINENT</small>   <small>CONTINENT</small>

<small>(+1 for Europe or Australia, +2 for Asia, +3 for South America, +5 for Africa)</small> because I had al-

ways been obsessed with it.

My study-abroad experience was intense. I barely learned any-

thing, but I traveled so much and met this amazing _____ from
<small>BOY/GIRL</small>

_____ <small>(+1 for Europe or Australia, +2 for Asia, +3 for South America, +5 for Africa)</small>
<small>CONTINENT</small>

and we had a short but beautiful relationship. I acquired a taste

for _____ <small>(+1 for food, +2 for alcohol)</small> and cannot wait to go
<small>SUBSTANCE</small>

back to try it again.

After graduation I took a year off to _____ <small>(+1 for work</small>
<small>ACTIVITY</small>

<small>abroad, +1 for travel, +3 for volunteer/Peace Corps)</small>. It was incredible, I learned so

much about myself and about life.

THREE OPTIONS HERE:

Option A

When I finished, there was no doubt in my mind that I was

going to move to _____ to try to make it in
_{CITY}

_____.
_{ARTISTIC PROFESSION}

Option B

After the year off I started law school at _____,
_{UNIVERSITY}

with plans to move to _____ immediately upon
_{CITY}

graduation.

Option C

I started working at a _____ as soon as I got
_{COMPANY}

back, but soon realized that I was not cut out for working a

9-to-5, so I went back to graduate school for _____.
_{SUBJECT}

RETURN

Living in _____ was not easy at first. I had al-
_{CITY}

most no friends and was paying way too much for my crappy

apartment. But I started to get the hang of it, and soon I had

met someone special at _____ (+1 for yoga, +1 for bar, +1 for
_{PLACE}

concert, +2 for political rally, +3 for Whole Foods, +5 for coffeeshop).

We started dating and eventually moved in together. We would

get married, but we refuse to do it until our gay friend

_____ (+1 for each additional name) is afforded the same
_{NAME}

right.

We got a really nice place in an up-and-coming neighborhood and adopted a rescue dog we named _____ (+3 if
NAME
named after musician). We did a total renovation on the place and installed _____ (+5 for hardwood floors, +4 for new lighting, +3 for stainless
HOME IMPROVEMENT
steel applicances), which was a great decision. We spend all our time in the kitchen cooking with fresh produce from _____
FOOD SOURCE
(+1 for farmer's market, +1 for Whole Foods, +5 for own garden), and we cannot live without our _____ (+5 if Italian-made).
APPLIANCE
It's been incredible. We usually spend Sunday mornings at home reading the *Times,* but on Saturdays we go to this great breakfast place called _____ (+5 if vegan).
NAME
Actually, last Saturday was especially amazing. We did breakfast and later went out to our favorite restaurant for dinner. Usually on weekends we like to try out new restaurants; our current favorite is this hole-in-the-wall _____ place (+5 if in bad
NATIONALITY
neighborhood). We haven't seen a white person in there since we started going, so we know it's authentic. It's fantastic.
Then after dinner we met up with our _____
NATIONALITY
friend(s) (+0 for American, +1 for European or Australian, +2 for Asian, +3 for South American, +5
for African) for a film at the _____. It was fantastic—you
ART HOUSE CINEMA
really have to put it in your Netflix queue. The film really moved me and got me thinking about my life. Lately I've been thinking of opening a _____ (+1 for bakery, +2 for restaurant, +3 for record label)
BUSINESS
or finishing my _____ (+1 for novel, +2 for PhD, +3 for mural, +5 for
CREATIVE ENDEAVOR
sculpture). I know it would be a risk, but I have to follow my dreams.

San Francisco

San Francisco is one of the top U.S. destinations for white people in terms of both travel and living. It is universally agreeable and is a safe discussion topic for any situation.

White people like to vacation in San Francisco because it has beautiful architecture and fantastic food and it is near the water. They like to live in San Francisco because of its abundance of nonprofit organizations, expensive sandwiches, and wine; its political outlook; and, most important, its diversity.

Since many white people either live in, plan to move to, or closely identify with San Francisco, it is imperative that you know how best to deal with them.

The city of San Francisco has a very multicultural population that ranges from white to gay to Asian. Within white culture this is known as "ideal diversity," since it both provides exotic restaurants and preserves prop-

erty values. The presence of gays and Asians is imperative, as it provides two of the key resources most necessary for white success and
happiness.

However, it is important to be aware of the fact that regions outside
San Francisco feature many people who are not white, gay, or Asian.
They are greatly appreciated during the census, but white people are
generally very happy that they stay in places like Oakland and Rich-
mond. This enables white people to feel good about living near people
of diverse backgrounds without having to directly deal with trouble-
some issues like income gaps or failing schools.

Still, the presence of other minorities is welcomed by white people
for so many more reasons than just statistics! Much in the way that
white people in Brooklyn feel a strong and unfounded connection with
the Notorious BIG, white people in San Francisco feel the need to
identify with rappers from the East Bay. Interestingly enough, the far-
ther they venture from San Francisco, the stronger their need to repre-
sent their region.

"Oh man, I went to the Too Short show last night. So hyphy man,
so hyphy. You should come by sometime and we'll ghost-ride the
Prius."

When you are presented with statements like this, the best response is to say, "Berkeley is close to Oakland," and the white person
will likely nod and throw up some sort of West Side hand sign.

Though it is exceptionally easy to put someone from San Francisco
in a good mood, there are some caveats. When talking to a white person who lives in San Francisco, it is best not to bring up New York City.
Though they live in a world-class city, San Franciscans have a crip-
pling inferiority complex about New York, and even hinting at that will
make them very sad or very defensive.

Fortunately, there is a foolproof method for quickly returning the
conversation to a positive, trust-building tone. No matter how much
you have offended someone from San Francisco, you can always
make them feel better by asking how they feel about Southern California. They will instantly talk of how it is filled with crime, pollution, hege-
monic culture, and the wrong kind of white people: "I swear California

is like two separate countries. I am so thankful that I live in the cultural center of the West Coast." This will allow them to reassert their superiority and leave the conversation with a positive feeling about themselves and about you.

Music Piracy

White people have always been renowned for having ridiculously large music collections. So when file sharing gave white people a chance to acquire all the music they ever wanted, they felt as though it was an earned right and not a privilege.

When (not if) you see a white male with a full iPod, ask him if all of his music is legal. If he does not immediately launch into a diatribe about his right to pirate music, you might have to nudge him a bit by saying, "Do you think that's right?" The response will be immediate and uniform. He will likely rattle off statistics about how most musicians don't make any money from albums, that it all comes from touring and merchandise. So by attending shows, he is able to support the musicians while simultaneously striking a blow against multinational corporations. He will proceed to walk you through the process of how record labels are set up to reward the corporation and fundamentally rob the artist of

their rights, royalties, and creativity. Prepare to hear the name Steve Albini a lot.

Advanced white people will also talk about how their constant downloading of music makes them experts who can properly recommend bands to friends and co-workers, thus increasing revenues and exposure. So, in fact, their "illegal" activities are the new lifeblood of the industry.

When they have finished talking, you must choose your next words wisely. It is considered rude to point out the simple fact that they are still getting music for free. Instead you should say, "Wow, I never thought of it like that. You know a lot about the music industry. What bands are you listening to right now? Who is good?" This sentence serves two functions: it helps to reassure the white person that they are your local "music expert," something they prize. Also, it lets them feel as though they have convinced you that their activities are part of a greater social cause and not simple piracy.

If you bring up this issue with a white person who says, "Nah, bro, I don't give a shit, Dave Matthews has enough money as it is," you are likely dealing with the wrong kind of white person.

In the even rarer situation where someone says, "It's all paid for, and it's all transferred from vinyl," you have found an expert-level white person and must tread carefully.

Because of the availability of music online, a very strict social hierarchy has been created within white culture whereby someone with a large MP3 collection is considered "normal," a large CD collection is considered to be "better," and a person with a large vinyl collection is recognized as "elite." These elite white people abhor the fact that music piracy has made their B-sides, live performances, and bootlegs available to the masses. Their entire life's work has been stripped of its rarity in terms of both object and sound on the record. The best thing you can say to them is "Vinyl still sounds better."

However, it is recommended that you do not let this conversation drag on much longer. If you let them continue, they are likely to spend hours talking to you about bands you've never heard of and to provide you with a weekly mix CD of rarities that you do not want.

Rugby

If you've been in a white person's apartment or home you might have noticed a ball that looks like a cross between an egg and a football. It is a rugby ball. This is an important sport for white people.

They love rugby for a number of reasons, the first of which is the fact that it is not very popular in North America. In fact, it is even less popular than soccer, which gives a white person that all-important edge in the contest to see who likes the most obscure sport. Though this is important, it is not the real reason why white people love the sport so much.

Rugby's greatest appeal lies in its uniforms. Unlike other sports, where jerseys are made out of nylon or mesh, rugby jerseys are like thick sweatshirts with collars! In fact, there is no other jersey on earth that can move so seamlessly from the playing field to the farmer's market.

Many white people first acquire a love of rugby during their high school and college years by playing either for a school team, or in the case of highly advanced white people, part of an intramural league. In fact, many white people will continue to play the sport into their early thirties at local parks on Saturday mornings. If you are looking to expand your group of white friends, you would be wise to get yourself invited to one of these games. However, you should be prepared to have your crotch grabbed.

Though playing the sport is the most common way for white people to become interested in rugby, a great number of them pick up a taste for the game while studying abroad in Australia or New Zealand. Like soccer, it gives them the chance to purchase a scarf of their adopted team, but more important, they can acquire a rugby jersey. Unlike a soccer scarf, this garment can be worn all year long, which provides for a more reliable trinket that can be used to initiate conversations about their time down under. For extra credit, some white people will declare that they are into Australian Rules football and not rugby. If you wish to befriend this person, it's best to ask them about the differences in rules, because they will be thrilled to tell you.

Aside from playing the game with white people, there is one other surefire way to use rugby for your personal gain. If you have determined that the white person you are talking to prefers rugby over soccer, it is strongly advised that you say, "You know, American football players might be bigger, but rugby players are so much tougher." Their response will be to tell you about how football players are weak because they wear pads. This will be followed by a knowing nod or wink in your direction and an invitation to join them for a game on the weekend.

New Balance Shoes

Because white-people tastes in shoes can change so quickly, it's not recommended that you ever talk to one about shoes. Over the years they have embraced (and eventually disowned) Uggs, Birkenstocks, Earth Shoes, and, most recently, Crocs. If a brand is popular, the chances are that the clock is ticking down to its imminent doom. One mention of your affinity for such footwear could undo all your hard work.

There is, however, one exception: New Balance running shoes. All white people own a pair! Seriously, the next time you are at a casual party where guests are encouraged to take off their shoes, take a look by the door at the veritable rainbow of New Balance sneakers.

But why do white people love them so uniformly? It is pretty simple, really. A few years ago it came out that Nike (and other manufacturers) were producing their shoes in Asian sweatshops and then selling them for a very high profit margin. White people were outraged; they generally prefer that children in developing nations first finish high school before working in shoe-producing sweatshops. Otherwise they might look foolish when their co-workers are talking about *The Catcher in the Rye.*

This enormous guilt over child labor meant that white people started to stop wearing Nike shoes. Subsequently, they were left to find a company that used fair labor practices to make shoes for the sports that they loved most: jogging, hiking, cross-country running, marathons, walking, and being seen in retro sneakers.

With factories in New England (include three in Maine!) and an extensive lineup of shoes that were meant only for running, New Balance was in the ideal position to both produce and distribute a product to the lucrative markets of white people conveniently located in the region. They quickly spread nationally and joined outdoor performance clothes as an essential part of the white uniform.

When you meet a person wearing New Balance shoes it is a good idea to ask about the marathon for which they are inevitably training. If they say, "I'm not training for a marathon," this is a good opportunity to raise your status by saying, "Oh, I thought only runners wore those. My running club all wear New Balance except for a few jerks who won't shut up about Asics. I'm still a bit sore from the ten-K run this morning."

This is an extremely effective move, since white people who jog are generally viewed as being better than white people who don't. Although perhaps it's more accurately stated that white people who jog feel the need to constantly prove they are better than white people who don't.

Note: It is considered a legendary white-male move to play basketball in a pair of New Balance. Lots of layups.

 # Beards

The popularity of beards with white people can fluctuate depending on the decade, but it always maintains a level of respectability regardless of current styles. Beards have been in fashion with white people since the dawn of white people. However, for research purposes, the modern white beard emerged at the same time as the modern white person: the '60s.

Over the next twenty years the beard would be strongly adopted by both rock stars and professors. For a white person, these are two of the most respected professions, so the ability to resemble either is seen as a very desirable trait.

By the '80s thick beards started to fall slightly out of favor and were limited mostly to graduate students and hobos, with the latter often having neater and better maintained facial hair. It was during this time that Don Johnson perfected the stubble look, which is like a regular beard but cut in such a way as to look like you haven't shaved for a few days. It was a success with white people since it was another case of having to do a lot of work to look like you didn't do any.

The '90s were not kind to beards, and the few practitioners were often white high school seniors who were into classic rock and "being wacky." Some would continue the beard into college, but they were the exception and not the rule.

At some point during the early part of the twenty-first century, white people discovered that the combination of a beard and thick-framed glasses (see #140, Glasses) was a solid white look that showed individuality, musical taste, and a rich educational pedigree. Bearded white males have had much social success in recent years, as their facial hair says, "Look at me. I am manly enough to grow this beard, yet I wear glasses, which shows my intellectual and sensitive side. I wear plaid, which shows I'm down with the people, but I also have expensive jeans, which shows that I have taste. I am the perfect male with whom to engage in a one-to-two-year relationship that might include living together. Allow me to buy you a Pabst." They are pretty much unstoppable.

In fact, the only white person who can top a bearded male is a white person who has grown ironic facial hair. These are the elite. They grow mustaches in various guises to show that they are so out of style that they are actually cooler than you. If one of these males is interested in the same person as you, it's best to back off. They call their own shots.

However, the ones with ironic facial hair make up only a small fraction of white people. The beards are still the most common and cohesive group.

Meeting a white male with a beard can be quite an experience. A good way to break the ice is to say, "I find that people with beards often grow them because they are hiding something. Is that the case with you?" The white person will laugh, and if they are interested in you romantically they will cleverly respond by saying, "Maybe I am, but it will take more than a question to uncover my secrets." If this happens you are dealing with a very smooth white operator.

If they respond by asking you questions about what you've heard in regard to their secrets as they clutch a black notebook, you are probably talking with a person who has a beard because they forgot to shave for six months.

Having Children in Their Late Thirties

Of the white people who want to have children, virtually all of them believe that they will be parents between the ages of 35 and 40.

Raising a white child is not easy, and it requires an exceptional amount of money and paraphernalia. Because of this, white people believe that it is impossible to properly raise children in their twenties. This period of their life is generally devoted to living in a big city, finding a spouse, starting a career, and purchasing their first piece of residential property.

By the time white people have entered their late thirties, they have often acquired enough capital to afford a larger property in an acceptable neighborhood (suburbs are acceptable, but frowned upon), tuition for a private school, and the series of accessories and specialists needed to ensure that the formative years of their white child will ensure future success and acceptance into an excellent university.

It is also universally recognized within white culture that the late thirties represents the time when personal journeys of self-discovery and therapy have reached a point where a white person is in the right frame of mind to raise a child.

If you encounter a white person who is trying to produce a child in their late thirties and is having some difficulty, it is very important that you never ever mention that it might be due to their trying to have children so late in life. Some better suggestions include "Did you smoke when you were younger?" or "How long have you been eating organic-only food?"

However, there are some exceptions to this rule. In recent years, a number of white women have become obsessed with the idea of being "hot moms" and are having children in their late twenties so that they can check it off the life list of accomplishments and return to their journey of personal discovery.

Red Hair

White people with red hair are one of the rarest types of white people that you can encounter. Their hair color was created by a northern European mutation that will likely be extinct in the next hundred years. Enjoy them while you can!

The role that red hair plays in white culture is not necessarily essential to understanding white people, but it is helpful. Aside from the obvious fact that white people have red hair, it occupies an interesting place of envy, mockery, and heritage.

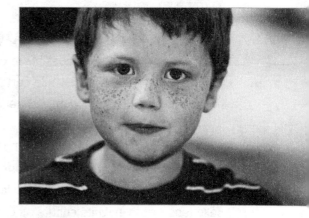

White people associate red hair with Irish roots, and allows redheads to constantly remind others that they have an "ethnic" heritage.

For white women red hair is seen as being highly desirable, with 1980s Molly Ringwald and Julianne Moore being the most popular redheaded heroines. Virtually every white woman you encounter will be able to tell you a story about how they have dyed or plan to dye their hair red at some time. This is because red hair is seen as both natural and not mainstream, two things that are highly coveted by all white people.

There are few positives for white men with red hair. They actually spend the majority of their lives dealing with the drawbacks of having red hair. These challenges emerge first during childhood, when it is common practice for white people to tease redheaded children (especially those with freckles). It is for this reason that all white people love any joke with the punchline "like a redheaded stepchild."

For example, when talking to a white person about an upcoming sporting event, try saying, "We are going to beat that other team like a redheaded stepchild." You will likely receive either a laugh or a knowing nod that you share their sense of humor.

In a situation where you need to befriend a white person, though it might be a bit presumptuous, it is considered acceptable form to greet a redheaded person by saying, "I had a rough childhood, too." At first the redhead will be taken aback, but soon they will tell you all about how they were taunted mercilessly in middle school as people demanded to know and/or made up songs about the color of their pubic hair.

98 Noam Chomsky

If it were possible to dole out white sainthood, Noam Chomsky would certainly be one of the first people to receive the honor, along with Michael Stipe and Conan O'Brien.

Though Chomsky has long been a hero to white people for his work in linguistics, he entered into the rarefied air of white history with the publication of *Manufacturing Consent: The Political Economy of the Mass Media* (1988), co-written with Edward Herman. It is universally recognized in white culture as one of the key sources of all knowledge about the media and the power structure of the United States.

It is strongly recommended that you read this book, but remember, you do not need to read the entire book in order to impress white people. For maximum results with minimum effort, it is advised that you closely read one chapter and then quote directly from it whenever you are given the chance.

When you feel as though you are
very comfortable with that chapter, you
can move on to the advanced activity of
telling a white person that they have "a
rather basic understanding of Chomsky." They will likely fight back, trying to
save face by refuting your claim, but
stand your ground. So long as you appear unshakable in your stance that
they are wrong, they will back down.
This is because deep down, white people are petrified that their understanding
of cultural theorists is flawed.

Note: This method of reading a single chapter and posing as an expert will work with any theorist, the more obscure the better.

99 Non-Motorized Boating

White people often find their greatest moments of
happiness near or in bodies of water. Rather than
simply splash around and enjoy the day, they often seek out as many
activities as possible that can enhance their water experience. Though
swimming is an old favorite, few white people are willing to take vacations just for the opportunity to swim. No, when white people need to
really enjoy the water, they get in a boat.

For white people, boating is like being able to camp on the water:
you get to spend a lot of time either alone or with a few close friends,
you have very little food, you might need to be rescued, and there is a
reasonable chance that you might die at the hands of Nature.

The type of boat enjoyed by a white person can vary greatly by location and attitude. For example, white people who live near an ocean
traditionally enjoy sailing, those near rivers prefer kayaking and rafting,

and those near lakes generally enjoy rowboats and canoes. However, these are only preferences, and it is possible for any white person in any given location to enjoy one or all of these activities. Boats with

motors are considered to be too popular with the wrong kind of white people and as such are not considered to be of any real value.

When you find out which type of boating a white person enjoys, your first instinct will be to search for some way to bring it up in conversation so that they will begin to trust you. But be absolutely careful: if you ask too many questions about boating, you are likely to be asked to join them "on the water sometime." This is your one-way ticket to being trapped with them for hours with no escape and an expectation that you will row/paddle/help with the sails.

100 The Boston Red Sox

Though many would argue that the Chicago Cubs (see #30, Wrigley Field) are the top club for white people, the Boston Red Sox remain the undisputed white franchise. In fact, were it not for the players, there would be no recorded instances of a person of color wearing a Boston Red Sox jersey.

White people love the Red Sox for a number of very important reasons, one of which is the fact that they play in Fenway Park, one of baseball's oldest and most iconic stadiums. This is viewed as the professional-sports equivalent of living in a Victorian house or a converted loft, both of which are highly desirable in the white community.

Though they are officially named the Boston Red Sox, the team is beloved by all of New England, including the popular white-people states of Maine, Vermont, and New Hampshire. This gives them more white coverage than any other franchise in baseball, beating out the Seattle Mariners.

Sadly, in 2004 the Boston Red Sox won the World Series and in the process lost something more highly prized by white people than success: character. Prior to that date the franchise was afflicted with the "Curse of the Bambino," brought on when a cheap owner sold Babe Ruth to the Yankees in 1920. The loss was a great one for white people, who for almost a century would tell it to anyone who would listen.

When dealing with a Red Sox fan, it is not hard to start a pleasant conversation. Just mention the team and they will likely tell you stories about how much they love the Red Sox and how the team used to break their heart every year. In fact the only ways you can upset a Red Sox fan are by mentioning that you like the Yankees or that they were the last Major League franchise to integrate. But mentioning you like the Yankees is still worse.

101 Scarves

White people's body temperatures do not operate on logical or consistent principles, and because of this white people are often forced to wear clothing combinations that may seem strange or illogical. One popular example is the performance vest, which solves the age-old problem of cold chest/hot arms. Another common combination is shorts and a sweat-shirt, which helps bring about comfort when your upper body is chilly but your lower half is sweltering. But without a doubt, the one piece of clothing that helps to regulate white body temperature in all situations is the scarf.

During winter months, it's no surprise to find white people all bundled up with scarves around their necks—it just makes sense. But

even as the weather warms up and the other layers start to fall off, the scarf remains.

It is not uncommon to see a white person in jeans, a sweater, and a scarf. In fact, it's not a rare occurrence to see a white person in a T-shirt, jeans, and a scarf. That's right: a thin cotton T-shirt paired with a scarf to enable maximum temperature control in bars and places with air-conditioning.

But not all white people wear the scarves for temperature reasons. A well-made scarf can be an essential part of a white person's ensemble, allowing for the all-important differentiation from other white people wearing the exact same clothes, and thus enabling one to be picked out of a crowd for dating or mocking purposes.

"I like the guy with the glasses in the white American Apparel shirt."

"Which one? There are eight."

"The guy with the kaffiyeh."

"Oh yeah, you're right. He does look smarter and more political than the other guys. He's clearly more sensitive to wind, so he's probably more sensitive in general. You should totally date him."

In addition to making up a key part of the white person's wardrobe, scarves also function as a vital pillar of the white gift economy. Knitted scarves can be created with relative ease, so many white people (especially women) like to knit them for friends and lovers. For this reason

alone, if you find yourself needing a new scarf but not a long-term relationship, dating a white woman might be the easiest and most cost-
effective solution.

Cleanses

In many cultures when someone does not eat
any food for days and survives only on a mixture
of water, cayenne pepper, and maple syrup they are said to be in the
midst of a "famine." But when a white
person does it, they are in the midst of
a "cleanse."

When white people are unable to
blame their parents for their problems,
they blame food additives. In fact, whenever a white person is feeling tired or
depressed it is almost always linked to
some sort of preservative in the food
they eat. When this happens to a white
person who only eats organic food, then
the water or air supply can be easily
substituted.

The only solution is to undergo a cleanse, whereby a white person
will spend more than ten days consuming only a liquid mixture of
water, lemon juice, cayenne pepper, and maple syrup. During this
process they will tell you how much more energy they have and how
great they feel. They are also likely to mention how their common ail-
ments (pimples, back pain, insomnia) have all magically disappeared.

White people generally believe that these cleanses are a lot like
doing a clean reinstall of the operating system on your computer: you
get rid of the things you don't want and you have a brand-new chance
to start over and use only open-source or web-based software. In both

cases you eventually slip back into bad habits and are likely to lose a few things you actually needed along the way.

Unfortunately the more "open" white people are likely to tell you exactly what has come out of them during the cleansing process: "Black liquid, like concentrated evil!" or "It looked like pantyhose filled with sausage." They will also tell you how their body is breaking down and passing all the toxins of the past six months or year.

If you are roped into one of these conversations, it's important you understand that white people are just looking to be told that they are being very healthy, or at least healthier than you. As such, the best response is to say, "Wow, I wish I had the willpower. I'm probably going to die at forty-five." This will reaffirm that they are healthier than you and are more likely to live forever.

Self-Deprecating Humor

Every white person you meet thinks they are smarter than everyone they know. Because of this, there is nothing they hate more than someone who outwardly tries to prove that fact. Instead, they much prefer when people make jokes about themselves in an attempt to appear outwardly inferior. Within white culture, the ability to laugh at yourself is considered on par with your ability to recommend restaurants. In other words, it's very important.

As with so many other things on this list, it's another situation where white people are able to score a double victory. Often, by putting themselves down they are also secretly insulting the person they are speaking to. For example, when white people attempt to put themselves down by making a joke around working too hard and not having a social life, they are saying that anyone who does have a social life is probably working less than them. If a white person is a self-proclaimed "nerd," all jokes around the topic are essentially their opportunity to say that they are smarter than you.

On the issue of money, if white people make jokes about not having any money, they are secretly criticizing those with money for not trying to be an artist or working for a nonprofit organization.

Within modern white society, this type of humor is considered essential for any sort of romantic success. When a white male says, "I'm so bad with girls, I think the Unabomber gets more girls than me. Do you remember that guy? I'll bet he at least gets letters in jail." If the woman he is talking to is even slightly interested, she will be drawn to him. White women prize the idea of a man who is confident enough to make jokes at his own expense. If she is not attracted to him, he can still win because she will want to set him up with other women who like men who make fun of themselves. He cannot lose.

Before you dive headfirst into the world of self-deprecating humor, it's important that you only make fun of things about you that don't really bother you. Making self-deprecating jokes about your family's history of lung cancer or your battle against painkiller addiction should only be done around expert-level white people. If done around regular-level white people, you will likely be considered a "weird downer."

On the whole, a good understanding of how to best put yourself down is essential to success in modern white situations.

104 Integrity

White people value nothing more in their musicians, artists, writers, directors, photographers, and publications than integrity. Many dictionaries define integrity as "a firm adherence to a code of especially moral or artistic values," but for white people, it can be more simply defined as "not selling out."

"Selling out" is when an artist succeeds to the point where they are paid for their work and are exposed to a larger audience. This creates two big problems for a white person, the most immediate of which is the fact that this artist will now be enjoyed by a diverse group of peo-

ple, including the wrong kind of white people. There is literally nothing more hated by white people.

Second, it serves as a reminder to the white person that he or she is not an artist. When white people like an artist who is not successful, they can enjoy the work knowing that they have more money and stability. They have made the more mature decision. When one of these artists succeeds and finds more money, it is a painful reminder of the sacrifice they made when they were younger. So when one of these artists succeeds, the only recourse that a

white person has is to say "They sold out."

When a white person says this around you, it is important that you do not say, "I wish we all had the integrity to be an associate copy-writer. It takes guts." Instead, it's recommended that you either relate a story about an artist you used to like, or move the conversation toward a discussion about what you would do if you were offered the opportunity to sell out. If you are eager to impress this white person, say that you would take the money, then allow the white person to tell you how they would never put a dollar sign on their art. This will provide them much-needed comfort as they begin the long process of finding a new obscure artist to temporarily enjoy.

105 Pretending to Be a Canadian When Traveling Abroad

There are bits of advice that are universally distributed by white people: "Eat organic," "Follow your dreams," "Buy property." But perhaps the one tip that all white people will pass on at some point is "Sew a Canadian flag on your backpack."

The years following World War II have not been kind to the reputation of Americans. Often they are seen as boorish, loud, obnoxious, and uncultured. As such, they are seen as unworthy of proper service and access to the "most authentic" parts of a country.

At some point in the past twenty years, some American white people abroad likely saw a local yelling at another white person. After a few minutes the person pointed to their "Roots" shirt and the flag on their backpack and said, "But I'm Canadian," whereupon the local's frown was turned upside-down. The Canadian was then granted

access to some sort of secret restaurant where they were served food that was so fresh, so local, and so authentic that it would be impossible to re-create anywhere else on Earth. This gave the Americans an idea. They sewed Canadian flags on their backpacks and watched the world open up to them.

The solution was perfect, since pretending to be Canadian required only a slight accent tweak (if any) and passing knowledge of a Canadian city. The latter was, and still is, far more difficult. Since that fateful time, anytime an American white person goes abroad they are likely to have a friend or relative tell them, "Pretend you're Canadian."

It also provides you with the best opportunity to earn the friendship of a white person. As soon as you find out that they are taking an extended vacation through Europe, Asia, or South America, go online and purchase a Canadian flag patch. Give this patch to the white person and you are sure to be included on mass e-mails and will likely receive some sort of trinket when they return.

Note: Canadian white people are given Canadian flag patches when they apply for their passports.

106 | The Criterion Collection

When a white person asks about your favorite film, you are really being asked whether or not you have taste. The second you open your mouth and mention a title, they will immediately pass judgment on you.

Choosing the right film can be tough. If you choose something that is too obscure or foreign you will be viewed as a threat, but choosing something too mainstream might make you look like a simpleton. The best thing you can do is to choose a film that is reasonably well known but is still considered artistic. Fortunately, there is a series of DVDs called the Criterion Collection that provides you with a handy list of films that are all acceptable to give as your favorite.

You might have noticed that many films are released in a regular edition and a Criterion Collection version. The latter is almost always more expensive, contains special features, and is conveniently packaged in a different way, which enables its owner to more easily display their superior knowledge of film.

If you tell a white person that you have recently purchased a DVD, nothing can deflate them faster than telling them you got the regular edition.

"I just bought *Rear Window*!"

"Criterion Collection?"

"No, the regular one."

"Oh."

Watch as their face drops along with their opinion of you. The only way to gain back their respect is to continually ask to borrow their Criterion copy of movies that you already own. This reminds them that they are more "into film" than you are, and you need them to help you figure out the correct way to entertain yourself.

107 Natural Childbirth

The early years of a white person are exceptionally important. The severity and frequency of problems during this era can be directly tied to the amount of therapy and counseling required later in life. Because of this, white people are trying to do whatever they can to keep their children natural and happy, and this begins at birth.

In spite of thousands of years of human history, white people like to believe that they are the first person ever to have a child. Or at least the first to have a truly gifted, beautiful child. For white people, birthing is now a spiritual experience that must be treated appropriately. This means candles, water, doulas, and relaxing music. Modern white birth is essentially an extreme yoga class with more screaming, and it only ends when a child pops out.

This also means that the birth should take place without the aid of pain-relief drugs. It is essential that white children are born into a completely drug-free environment. This ensures that they will have a more powerful experience when they start taking drugs in high school.

When the birth is complete, everyone is left with a child, the smell of incense, self-satisfaction, and a placenta. Normally everything but the placenta will remain, but in recent years white people have started

the interesting practice of eating this piece of afterbirth. Though theoretically this is cannibalism, many white people view it as the best in organic food. This is because during pregnancy white women will not eat sushi, drink alcohol, smoke, dye their hair, or engage in any other activities that might endanger the child. The result is an allegedly delicious, organic, grain-fed placenta. It is unknown whether it is acceptable for vegans to eat this.

After learning that a white person is pregnant, it is a good idea to provide a list of recipes for placenta. Even if they do not plan to eat the placenta, they will view you as progressive and open to new things. If you can fake a recipe from your own culture, it is a certainty that the white person will use it, even if they were not planning on it. Other acceptable gifts include candles, a baby sling, and/or a *Nature Sounds* CD.

108 High School English Teachers

Though white parents do a good job of introducing their children to culture, literature, and creative writing, they can only take them so far before the inevitable rebellion sets in at 12 or 13. At this point, the parents must hand off their child to a high school English teacher, who is responsible for educating the child in literature, art, creative writing, and New York City.

Many white people will have up to four different high school English teachers during high school, so how do they choose the "one"? While you would think that this is a complicated procedure requiring the forging of a deep bond, ungraded poetry, and the lending of extracurricular books, it really isn't so complicated. The way that a white person identifies the "chosen one" is dependent entirely on who guides them through *The Catcher in the Rye.* Simple as that.

The high school English teacher is instrumental in leading white people toward arts degrees and eventually careers in law, nonprofit, and media, or as high school English teachers. The latter course represents the "white circle of life."

The importance of high school English teachers goes far beyond everyday life. They have inspired such classic films as *Freedom Writers, Dangerous Minds,* and *Dead Poets Society.* In fact, white people are so convinced that teaching high school English can make a difference that the U.S. government created "Teach for America" to accommodate the overwhelming demand from white people to teach underprivileged children about the importance of Faulkner.

But how is this information of any use in day-to-day dealing with white people? Its value is twofold. First, white people who are unhappy with their jobs will often say they wish to go to graduate school or to teach high school English. So whenever a white person is complaining to you about their job, giving them the advice to become a high school English teacher is always welcomed and appreciated. But most important, you can use this as an easy way to determine what type of white person you are dealing with. If you ask, "Who was your favorite teacher in high school?" and they respond "My gym teacher," then you are dealing with the wrong type of white person. If they say "math" or "science" you should investigate further to see if you are actually speaking with a white person.

Native Wisdom

We've already seen how white people love religions that their parents don't belong to, but that doesn't mean that they will only take life advice from that religion. White people all seek wisdom from anyone who is from a different culture. For over fifty years, the undisputed champion of wisdom has been the Native American.

White people are loath to convert to any set of beliefs that fails to blend in with modern furniture, so they will rarely align themselves as

Native American. However, they do appreciate the tips and advice passed on by Native American elders.

This advice is considered to be particularly powerful to white people who claim to have Native American ancestry. "The parable of the wolf and the hawk is particularly applicable to me since I'm one thirty-second Cherokee. It has really helped me to resolve the issues I've been having with my friend over whether or not it's ethically acceptable to eat vegan food cooked in pots that have touched meat. I am at one with him now."

If a white person ever tries to pass on Native wisdom to you, it is best that you nod in agreement. If they have Native ancestry, it's advised that you ask them a few questions about it.

110 Trying Too Hard

If you like something—anything—there is a 100 percent chance that there is a white person out there who likes it more than you. It doesn't matter what it is—Mandarin, sushi, marijuana, African music, hip-hop, television, Madagascar, or jai alai.

It is widely accepted that all white people feel the need to be an expert on something. Most white people will be satisfied with being recognized as the expert among their friends, but there are others who need to take it to an entirely different level. Encountering one of these people can be a jarring experience, and if you do not handle the situation just right you can quickly lose their friendship, or worse, appear arrogant to a group of white people.

The story is always the same. You will be in a group of people and casually mention something like "I really like Jimi Hendrix," then out of the corner of the room you will hear "What's your favorite album?" Just as you are preparing to give your answer, the person who asked will jump in with a rapid-fire series of questions: "Do you have *Loose Ends*? How much vinyl do you own? Did you get the bootlegs with B. B. King and Jim Morrison? Did you read *Electric Gypsy*?" and before you know it you are reeling and feeling as though you are the victim of some sort of inquisition. Your first reaction might be to call the person a nerd and tell them to "take it easy." Though that might bring about a short-term laugh from the group, it will engender hate and resentment from the white person you have burned.

In the rare instance where you feel as though your knowledge is on par, do not, under any circumstance, engage them. You cannot win.

Portland, Oregon

Portland, Oregon, is essentially a *Lord of the Flies* scenario with white people in the Pacific Northwest instead of children in the South Pacific. In both cases, we have a situation whereby a homogenous group of people is left alone in an area with no one to keep them in check. Eventually the euphoria and self-congratulation devolves into savagery and murder.

Statistically, Portland, Oregon, is the whitest metropolis in the United States, and unsurprisingly, it's also the most bike-friendly, vegan-friendly, GLBT-friendly city in America.

The low rents have made it highly desirable to freelance designers and artists, who no longer have to work 40-hour weeks to afford their lofts. Instead, they can use the rest of their time to focus on their art, check e-mail at local coffeeshops, and go to indie rock shows at the Crystal Ballroom.

But the appeal of Portland goes beyond the young. With affordable real estate prices, it attracts white people with children from Los Angeles, New York, Austin, Chicago, Boston, and San Francisco in droves. Each of them brings their own unique heritage, modern furniture, Prius, and recipe for vegetarian chili.

The city is expanding its bike lanes, adding to its light rail service, and registering more and more Democrats, and it is thriving. On the

Lord of the Flies timeline, Portland has not reached the stage where they smash Piggy's glasses, but there is a strong likelihood that the city will have mass riots and murder when the local grocery co-op runs out of organic wild salmon.

This knowledge is important, because whenever a white person complains about their city, you should always say, "Have you thought about moving to Portland?" This will comfort them as they tell you their plan to move there in a few years. But unless you make it clear that you are moving there to open some sort of ethnic restaurant, do not tell them that you plan to join them in the Rose City. It will make them uncomfortable.

112 | Free Health Care

In spite of having access to the best health in-surance and fanciest hospitals, white people are passionate about the idea of socialized medicine, so much so that they have memorized statistics and examples of how for-profit medi-cine has destroyed the United States.

Before you can exploit this information for personal gain, it's impor-tant that you understand why white people are so in love with free health care.

The first and most obvious reason is "They have it in Europe." White people love all things European, and this is especially true of things that are unavailable in the United States (rare beers, absinthe, legal marijuana, prostitution, soccer). The fact that it's available in Canada isn't really that impressive, but it does contribute to their will-ingness to threaten to move there.

These desires were only heightened in 2007 when Michael Moore released *Sicko,* a documentary that contrasts the health-care industry in the United States with those of Canada, France, and Cuba. As a general rule of thumb, white people are always extra passionate about

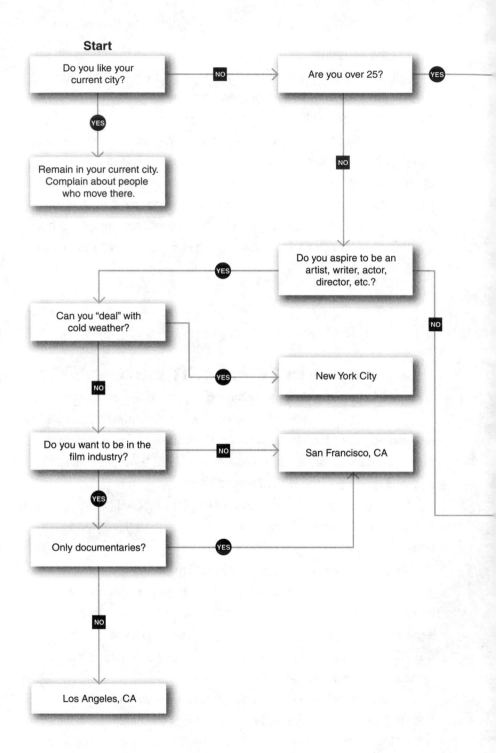

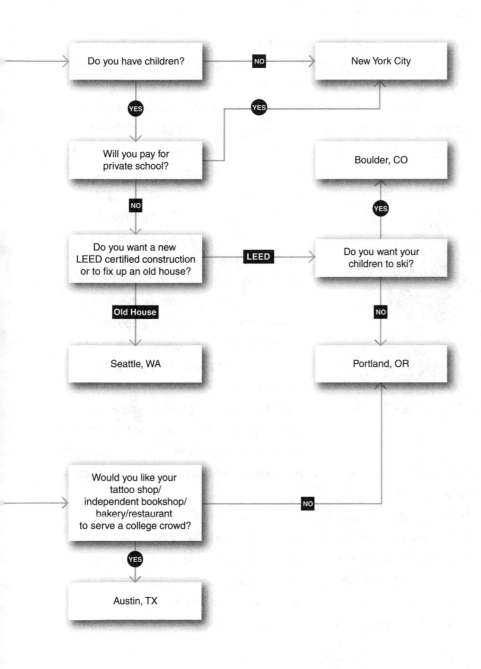

| Do you have children? | **NO** → | New York City |

YES ↓

| Will you pay for private school? | → **YES** → New York City |

NO ↓

| Do you want a new LEED certified construction or to fix up an old house? | **LEED** → | Do you want your children to ski? |

| Boulder, CO |

YES ↑ (from "Do you want your children to ski?")

Old House ↓

| Seattle, WA |

NO ↓ (from "Do you want your children to ski?")

| Portland, OR |

| Would you like your tattoo shop/ independent bookshop/ bakery/restaurant to serve a college crowd? | **NO** → Portland, OR |

YES ↓

| Austin, TX |

White Migration Logic

issues that have been the subject of a Moore documentary. As a test, ask them about 9/11, gun control, or health care and then say, "Where did you get that information?" You will not be surprised at the results.

But the secret reason all white people love socialized medicine is that they love the idea of receiving health care without having a full-

time job. This would allow them to work as freelance designers/consultants/copywriters/photographers/bloggers, open their own bookstores, stay at home with their kids, or be a part of Internet start-ups without having to worry about a benefits package. Though many of them would never follow this path, they appreciate having the option.

If you need to impress a white person, merely mention how you got hurt on a recent trip to Canada/England/Sweden and though you were a foreigner you received excellent and free health care. They will be very impressed and likely tell you about how the powerful drug and health-care lobbies are destroying everything.

Though their passion for national health care runs deep, it is important to remember that white people are most in favor of it when they are healthy. They love the idea of everyone having equal access to the resources that will keep them alive. At least until they have to wait in line for an MRI. This is very similar to the way that white people express their support for public schools when they don't have children.

113 | Che Guevara

Though he would likely hate them all, white people cannot get enough of Che Guevara. They love his radical politics, his fight for the peasants, and his role in establishing the Communist government of Cuba, which has found varying degrees of success since its inception.

But far and away his greatest contribution to white culture has been his ability to look good on a T-shirt.

Wearing a Che Guevara T-shirt tells the world that you are cool (it's a T-shirt), you are left wing (he was a Communist!) and you look good in red (the shirt is always red). For bonus points, some white people like to pair the Che T-shirt with a sport coat and a pair of jeans. It's the ultimate mix of business and peasant.

Though highly successful in T-shirt form, this has not been without problems. Many younger people are fairly confident that Che Guevara was created by the same guy who created Obey Giant.

Still, his dashing good looks and young death have made him a hero to upper-middle-class white people everywhere who hope to one day be able to pull off a beret in public.

When you encounter a white person with a Che T-shirt, it's very important to approach them with the following understanding. White people would fondly embrace a Communist revolution if they were given jobs as writers, artists, photographers, filmmakers, politicians, or architects. So long as they don't have to do manual labor, they share Che's utopian vision!

Follow that simple rule and you will likely find a T-shirt of your own waiting for you at your desk on International Workers' Day.

114 | *The New Yorker*

The magazine industry relies heavily on white people, not only for staffing but also for subscriptions. White people love many magazines, including *The Economist, Wired, Saveur, The Atlantic,* and *The Utne Reader.* But without fail, the magazine that will get you the most respect from white people is *The New Yorker.*

The magazine is made up of many sections: letters, cultural listings, snippets, and extremely long articles. Toward the end of the magazine you will notice ads for many things that white people like, including summer study programs, language software, and berets.

When you first pick up *The New Yorker,* you will notice that there are not a lot of pictures. This is very important to white people, as it makes them feel smarter about reading it. However, do not assume that white people read every word of *The New Yorker.* Due to an abundance of words and the fact that the magazine is published weekly, white people have been subscribing to and not reading *The New Yorker* for more than seventy years.

Every white person is ashamed about letting their copies of the magazine pile up, and this is your ticket to common ground.

Once you have successfully moved the conversation to a place where you can reference the magazine, it's a fantastic move to say, "I need to take a week off just so I can get caught up on the issues piling up next to my bed." Once the white person has realized that they are not alone, they will confess their shame to you and feel a deep connection.

Conversely, this information can be used to raise your status at the expense of another white person. Prior to meeting them, read one article in *The New Yorker,* paying extra attention to the end of the article (the part that is continued in the back). When you meet the white person, attempt to engage them about this part of the article and ask them questions. Be prepared for the white person to lie or try to change the subject. Do not give up.

When it finally becomes obvious that they have not read it, try to be apologetic and pretend as though you honestly thought they had read it and you didn't mean to call them out. This will show the rest of the group that you are kind but also smarter than the person you just burned.

115 Non-American News Sources

White people love to talk about the news. It is an excellent way for them to show off how knowledgeable they are about current affairs. If you plan on spending large amounts of time with white people you will be expected to have some understanding of current events and strong opinions about them. Of course, you will be expected to initiate and back up your salient points with evidence from a reputable news source.

News sources are ranked on a strict hierarchy, and your choice in the matter can be the difference between respect and mockery. Generally speaking, foreign news sources cannot be topped in terms of quality and status. The British Broadcasting Corporation (BBC) is the gold standard since it's foreign, available on PBS, and focused strictly on international news (always the best). If a white person starts talking about a "piece they saw on the BBC about Sumatra," it can be almost impossible to trump them. However, there is an ace in the hole that should only be used in emergencies—when respect and status lie in the critical balance.

If you can properly cite a foreign news source in a foreign language you will be viewed in the highest regard. "Oh, that piece on the BBC was good, but I saw this amazing story on TV5/RTL/RAI/NHK that really opened my eyes on the subject. I have to pay an extra fifteen dollars a month for the channel, but it really is worth it. It's one of the few ways I can keep up my French/German/Italian/Japanese in this country."

A white person might respond by saying they do not own a TV, but that is essentially a last-ditch effort to save face.

A final note: If you do need to cite an American news source, CNN and MSNBC are acceptable, though not encouraged. Major networks such as ABC, NBC, and CBS are fairly neutral, although mentioning local news will speak poorly of your intelligence. Most important, if you even mention Fox News you will have lost respect and credibility to such a high degree that you might have to move.

In fact, it is a good idea to tell white people that you have called your cable company and asked it to remove Fox News from your programming package, and that it was done at a considerable cost.

Subtitles

We already know that film is very important to the cultural development of white people. So when you are talking to them about films, it's essential to understand a few rules.

The simplest rule to follow is that every foreign film is good. Amazingly, in the history of cinema, the only truly awful films ever produced have been in English. Any film that features subtitles is regarded as excellent since it is produced outside of the "Hollywood system," and therefore is more free to delve into real issues of modern life and unbridled artistic expression. There are no exceptions.

Be aware that if white people know your nation of ancestry, they will expect you to be familiar with the films of that nation. This has created a heavy burden on Asian people, especially the Chinese and Japanese. If you are able to recommend a film or director that is particularly obscure, a white person will imme-

I must avenge my father's death to put my inner turmoil to rest.

diately count you among their closest friends—but be prepared for when they get the director's entire catalog from Netflix and want to talk to you about it.

The best way to use this knowledge to your advantage is if you are trying to create a romantic relationship with a white person. Scan the paper for the foreign films playing at your local art-house theater, and suggest it as a possible date. The white person will be unable to turn you down, as rejecting you would be rejecting foreign film, and if you were to say, "Oh, you don't like foreign films? I'm sorry, I really misjudged you. Have fun at *Harry Potter*," their shame might be enough to propel the date into a full-scale relationship.

117 | Premium Juice

If you live in an area with a lot of white people and are looking for a way to make money, there are few sounder plans than to sell them premium juice. Yoga studios, organic co-ops, and breakfast places will all make money, but in terms of national franchising and profit margins, nothing can beat premium juice.

The white person's obsession with expensive juice has helped launch a number of prominent orange juice companies as well as breakfast places offering up $6 glasses of "fresh-squeezed" orange

juice. However, this has become so commonplace that there is no status associated with merely drinking juice from an orange.

The ideal white-person juice costs between $3 and $6, contains a blend of organic fruit, and is infused with some sort of vitamin or medicinal herb (echinacea is best). There are some instances where the juice is simply that of a single fruit, but in those cases it must be a fruit that seems difficult to juice—pomegranate, for example.

Traditional white medicine holds that drinking juice can cure and prevent colds. The potency of the juice is determined by its rarity and organicness, as well as the ecological commitment of the juice manufacturer. If you do not have time to investigate how each company produces its product, just buy the most expensive.

Aside from using this information to start a new business, it can be very useful in the office. If you are picking up lunch for a white person and they ask you to get them something to drink, bringing back an Odwalla or Naked Juice will be met with joy and awe. It will create the impression that you care about their health and do not spare any expense when it comes to workplace health. Also, the gift economy of the office dictates that this person must then get you a juice of equal or higher value when they purchase lunch. If they fail to do this within a week, you can point it out to other workers and slowly climb over them on the corporate ladder.

118 | The ACLU

Though white people are a fiercely independent group, there are certain organizations they depend upon to help protect their rights and freedoms: Greenpeace, MoveOn.org, the Electronic Frontier Foundation (EFF), and, most important, the American Civil Liberties Union (ACLU).

Perhaps one of the most universal things on this list is white people's love of the ACLU and its actions. And why not? It incorporates so many things that white people love: lawyers, religions their parents don't belong to, knowing what's best for poor people, non-profit organizations, and expensive sandwiches. (The last point is not confirmed, but it's a pretty safe bet to say that there is nothing ACLU lawyers like more than removing the Ten Commandments from public places and then digging into a nice panino.)

Though the stated goal of the ACLU is "to defend and preserve the individual rights and liberties guaranteed to every person in this country by the Constitution and laws of the United States," in recent years their top priority has been to protect white people from having to look at things they don't like. At the top of this list is anything that has to do with Christianity: Ten Commandments tablets, public signs that mention God or Jesus, nativity scenes, any sort of Christian statue. Though some would say this is because white people hate Christianity, that is not true. White people simply do not enjoy the aesthetics of Christian artifacts. They much prefer Hindu or Buddhist furniture and imagery, and generally consider Christianity to be a little trashy.

The ACLU also helps to defend the parts of the Bill of Rights that white people like (everything but the right to bear arms).

WARNING: When talking about the ACLU with white people, it is best not to point out any contradictions in their support of the organization, as this will anger and upset white people on a level you have never experienced.

Plaid

Unlike many of the things on this list, white people have not agreed to love plaid flannel blindly and in perpetuity. In fact, the past fifty years have seen the popularity of plaid ebb and flow like the tides at virtually the same level of predictability.

Much in the same way that the tides are tied to the moon, plaid is

tied very strongly to music. During periods when more folk-like or Country-Western music is popular, the torsos of white people will be decked out in some variety of plaid. The modern birth of flannel-based plaid occurred during the '70s when bands like the Byrds, the Grateful Dead, and the Eagles brought a Country-Western aesthetic to rock music. The current iteration has been

closely tied to the growth of a folksier blend of indie music.

However, the "grunge" era seems to poke a hole in this theory, as white people were wearing plaid and listening to music that was closer to punk than to folk music. There are two schools of thought on this issue. The first is that grunge served a folk-like function by providing a voice to a marginalized generation in the same way that Woody Guthrie did during the Depression. The other school of thought is

"Who cares about grunge? I thought Kurt Cobain wore sweaters and stuff." This era also featured a significant number of rappers and gang members wearing plaid, again adding to its status as an anomaly.

It is important to understand the role of plaid in white culture, because a lack of awareness could result in a major social mistake. You see, the wrong kind of white people have seen no ebb and/or flow in their love for plaid clothing. So depending on the position in the cycle, if you were to run into a Caucasian person in an airport wearing a plaid shirt, big belt buckle, raw denim, and some faded shoes, your first instinct might be "Oh, a white person. I'll tell him how much I like Brooklyn and Yeasayer so I can trade seats with him."

But be careful! You might be looking at the wrong kind of white person, who will probably be quite offended if you imply he's from San Francisco. The lesson here is that if you are not in a white enclave, it's best to assume that people dressed like farmers are farmers. This is not only to prevent offending the wrong kind of white person, but also, if you mistake a regular white person for a farmer, they will feel pretty good that they look authentic. You can't lose.

 **Platonic Friendships**

When you see a white woman and a white man eating dinner together, watching a movie, or drinking at a bar you probably think they are a couple. Not so fast! White people often engage in something called a "platonic friendship." These arrangements feature a white male who is in love with a white female who needs companionship or access to someone with a car.

The relationship is symbiotic for a long time as the white male believes he is making "progress" in his efforts to sleep with the white woman. The white female is in turn rewarded with companionship, someone to help her move, and an excellent "backup" plan in case she is unable to date the male of her choice. (Note: There are instances where the male and female roles are reversed, but these are far rarer.)

During these relationships both parties are required to pretend that the idea of them as a couple is absurd. This allows the male to complain to his friends about his unrequited love, while the female uses this strategy to attempt to ward off (or at least discourage) a sexual advance from the male.

Every single white person who has been in a platonic friendship has experienced at least one of three possible outcomes. The first and most hopeful is that the white male achieves his goal and is able to convince the white female to date him. This often happens after either a drunken sexual advance or, for the more sensitive males, a proclamation of love through a letter or poem. Once the female has agreed to a relationship, it just becomes a normal white relationship.

The opposite of this, of course, is when the female rejects the advance or declaration of love. In this horribly awkward situation, the white male will reassure her that everything is OK and then proceed to extricate himself from the friendship and begin the process anew with a different girl. While white girls will often complain about how they have lost so many friends because of this, they also like to say that these situations are "complicated" and are "a long story." In both cases, they are hoping you will ask them about it.

Finally, and perhaps most common, is the situation where the friendship becomes strained after the white female begins dating another male. The more aggressive white males might even be willing to profess their love at this stage in a Hail Mary attempt to reach their goal of romantic involvement. But in general, most white males will pretend to be happy for a while and then gradually stop talking to the female.

When you are talking to a white person about personal stuff, make up a story about how you were friends with a girl/guy when you were between 15 and 20 (these are the prime platonic years) and how you were obsessed with her/him; you had these great moments but she ended up dating some jerk who cheated on her/him. Your point will be to prove the lesson about the value of a sensitive person over a good-looking one. There is no chance you will even be able to finish this story, as the white person you are talking to will interrupt you to tell you their version of the story. All you need in order to seal the friendship is to nod and reaffirm how right they are.

121 Reusable Shopping Bags

Many white people have been able to decrease their carbon footprint by using plastic shopping bags for such diverse purposes as garbage bags and bathing-suit transport. Though helpful, the accumulation of bags is often at a much quicker pace than the reusing process, and within months, drawers and closets begin to fill up and are not emptied until the white person moves. It is one of the great tragedies of modern white culture. Fortunately, as with all white problems, there is a simple, expensive solution!

Advanced white people have started to reject plastic shopping bags and have started to bring their own bags to the supermarkets and stores that they frequent. These bags serve two essential purposes in white culture: marginally reducing waste and, more important, publicly showing a commitment to the environment.

Basic-level white people will use the free tote bag they received from their donation to public television or radio to carry a small amount of groceries or farmer's market produce back to their homes. Though this is respectable, it's not really all that impressive.

Up a notch are people who have purchased a bag that was specially designed for groceries and features the logo of the store on the side. This not only serves to show those outside the store that they shop at a responsible location, it tells the people in the store that they are lesser for not using that bag. This is essential for defining the hierarchy of white people within certain grocery stores. But again, this bag is only really useful for small quantities of groceries and produce.

The highest-ranking white people will only use the aforementioned bags for short trips. When they purchase large amounts of food they will bring their own bags made of organic cotton string. These bags expand and can accommodate more food and are easily loaded into the

 back of a Prius or Subaru. But even that is not enough. To achieve the highest possible status, white people must also carry their own muslin sacks that they can use to bag produce like tomatoes and garlic. This prevents them from using one more plastic bag, and it demands recognition from the person at the checkout counter.

All these white people want you to tell them that they are doing the right thing. In fact, they are so eager for praise that you might be able to acquire a free bag if you play your cards right. At the checkout counter of the organic coop, take a look to see if the white person in front of you has more bags than they need. If they do, nudge them and say "What are those?"—doing your best to get the white person to deliver a speech about how much waste is created by plastic bags. Then start to ask where to get them, and finally say, "I don't really have that much in my cart, and I'd really hate to have to use one of those plastic bags. I would feel guilty all day." And boom! Free bag! If you are willing to travel to different markets, you can likely acquire a full set within a month.

122 | Acoustic Covers

In terms of music, nothing will please white people more consistently than acoustic covers of songs that don't seem to lend themselves to acoustic covers. In fact, whenever a white person puts together a mix—on a CD, an mp3 set, or a podcast, or for a party—the crown jewel is always an acoustic cover of a pop or hip-hop song.

On the surface it may seem confusing that white people love these covers so much, but if you dig just below the surface, it's really not so surprising. You see, white people are not supposed to like mainstream hip-hop, pop music, or heavy metal—those are all enjoyed far too much by the wrong kind of white people. But because of their relative popularity, virtually all white people are familiar with the music. So when a musician takes one of those songs and converts it into an acoustic cover, they have made it acceptable for white people to enjoy because it is now in a style of music that they like.

White people love acoustic guitar, but they also love familiarity and catching pop-culture references, so when an acoustic cover comes along, it delivers on every level!

There is a 100 percent chance that at some point a white person will ask you to "come listen to this," and watch your face to see how long it takes you to figure out that the song is a cover. If you plan on pursuing friendship with this white person or if they have something you need, it would serve you well to act surprised when you recognize the song, then start laughing, then ask the white person, "Where did you get this?" They will gladly tell you and will be more likely to buy you lunch.

123 Dave Chappelle

Sitting next to the Michel Gondry collection on the DVD shelf of white people is *Chappelle's Show,* seasons one and two. Though Chappelle had been very popular with white people prior to getting his own show (ask a white person if they have seen *Half-Baked*), when he was given a weekly sketch show on Comedy Central it propelled him from preferred comic to true white comedic hero—joining '80s Eddie Murphy, early '90s Martin Lawrence, and late '90s Chris Rock.

Though Dave Chappelle is popular with all kinds of people, the way that he is popular with white people might be different from what you would expect. For one, you have to be careful about which sketch you list as your favorite, as some have fallen out of favor. When it was first shown, all white people laughed very hard at the whole "Rick James" bit, but within a month it had been strongly co-opted by the wrong kind of white people, who started saying, "I'm Rick James, bitch," in the

same way that they used to say "Yeeaaah, baby!" after watching *Austin Powers.* So to quote that sketch will likely identify you as someone who lives on the wrong side of good taste.

When the topic of Dave Chappelle comes up, it is recommended that you mention the show only sparingly. Instead, you should mention how much you loved his many stand-up specials. This will not only give the white person a chance to repeat some jokes to show their comedic timing, but it will allow them to tell you how they were really into Dave Chappelle's comedy before the show. Since you have mentioned the comedy specials, they will recognize you as someone who likes things before everyone else—quite the enviable position indeed.

If you are attempting to move your friendship with a white person to the next level (either socially or romantically), it is a good idea to invite them to your house to watch something featuring Dave Chappelle and smoke marijuana. This combination is irresistible to white people.

124 | Tibet

In the history of white causes, there might never be one bigger than Tibet. The cause has celebrity endorsements, concerts, T-shirts, bumper stickers, Buddhism, and a simple solution. The latter is the most important, since many white people do not need to know the history of the situation in order to be passionate about the need for China to "get out of Tibet." Unlike many other problems that have exceptionally complex solutions (global hunger, poverty, the environment), Tibet presents a rather clear-cut solution and is much easier to support blindly.

Ask a white person why they love Tibet so much and you will always get the same response: they see the nation as a place where people live simple lives, practice Buddhism, and find enlightenment on a daily basis. Tibetans have no need for material posessions, and it is rumored that the country actually absorbs pollution from China and turns it into self-help books for the West.

When it comes to the inhabitants of Tibet, white people are pretty sure that the entire nation is made up of cool Buddhist monks who know martial arts. These men are perhaps the most respected people in white culture after bicycle mechanics and indie rock musicians.

For these reasons, white

support of Tibet is absolute. It is scientifically impossible to meet a white person who doesn't support a free Tibet. This means that you have a subject that is guaranteed to get a favorable response from white people. If a conversation with a white person ever turns to politics and you are feeling slightly uncomfortable, it's best to immediately say, "Can you believe what's going on in Tibet?" Problem solved.

Also, if you are working in a predominantly white environment, it's probably best to put a "Free Tibet" bumper sticker on your car. It won't really open any doors, but it doesn't hurt.

Nintendo Wii

Video games play a very interesting role for white people. Many white males are very into the Xbox 360 or Playstation 3, on which they play games like Final Fantasy, Grand Theft Auto, Halo, Gears of War, and Rock Band. If they tell you that they play "a lot of Madden," you are speaking with the wrong kind of white person. However, on the whole white people have very specific tastes in the types of video games they like.

Almost all of them grew up playing Super Mario Bros. on the original Nintendo, and when you bring up the topic of modern video games they will almost always say, "They are too complicated now, I don't play them. Except for the Wii."

Launched in 2006, the Nintendo Wii has reignited white interest in video games. The Wii, which features motion controls, does not require any special skill beyond flailing your arms. The system also accommodates up to four players, meaning that it has become an excellent replacement for board games at dinner parties. White people are known to gather around the TV and spend hours playing Wii Bowling, Wii Tennis, or maybe even Mario Party.

The main reason the Wii has tapped into white culture is the creation of "Mii's." These are little avatars that can be used as characters within games. After spending most of their lives creating themselves through the purchase of haircuts, glasses, and tattoos and the growth of facial hair, white people love the idea of being able to re-create their "look" on the Wii. However, virtually all white Mii's end up the same—

white skin, glasses, and a choice of messy hair (male), long hair (female), bangs (female), or bald (male).

White people who do not own a Nintendo Wii especially enjoy telling people how much they want to get one. White people who do own Wii's quickly tire of them and only end up playing when friends come over.

If you know a white person with a Wii, it's never a good idea to buy them a game. Instead, you should try to get yourself invited over to play. They are desperate for the company.

126 Conspiracies

Conspiracies occupy a very interesting place among white people. They almost all believe in one conspiracy or another, but choosing the wrong conspiracy can make you look like an idiot while choosing the right one makes you look like a savvy revisionist historian.

Generally speaking, the type of conspiracy most beloved by white people involves the American government working with some sort of multinational corporation to extract money or resources from a poor nation. Any conspiracy involving Cuba, Central/South America, or Southeast Asia is generally acceptable. Your ability to back this up with any sort of book evidence will help to reinforce your status as a smart individual.

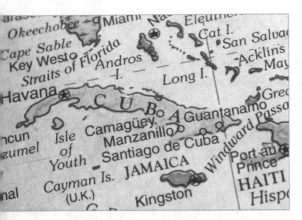

Conspiracies around 9/11, aliens, Jewish bankers, and the moon landing are generally frowned upon by white people, and your belief in their existence will get you labeled as an idiot; no matter how hard you try, it will be impossible to recover.

127 | *The Simpsons*

When searching for common ground with a white person, a mention of *The Simpsons* is a sure-fire bet to start a lively and engaging conversation. But simply stating that you like *The Simpsons* is a recipe for disaster. You have to be prepared to list the specific period in which you enjoyed the show or else you might be seen as someone with poor taste.

The Simpsons highlights the concept of "jumping the shark," which is one of the most important phenomena in white culture and one of the best methods for determining the cultural significance and knowledge of a white person.

"Jumping the shark" is a phrase that was coined after an episode of *Happy Days* in which Fonzie, a lead character, jumped over a shark. Many people point to that as the moment the show stopped being worth watching.

Ever since that time, white people have been obsessed with accurately noting the exact moment that something stopped being relevant. By being able to judge this with the most detail, a white person is able to be seen as a sharp critic of popular culture and one that deserves to be heard. But, as with everything in white culture, there are a lot of rules and you have to be careful about what you say.

If you choose to declare that something jumped the shark too early, you risk looking as though you are lying in an effort to seem smart. If you miss some key episodes you will be mocked as a snob who doesn't really understand the show or its values. For example, saying "I think *The Simpsons* jumped the shark after season two" will be met with laughter and taunts about your faux snobbery.

However, declaring that something jumped the shark too late will make you look uncultured in your taste for the show and you will lose all respect.

The safest route is to say, "I was obsessed with the first few seasons. My favorite episode is still 'Mr. Plow.'" But if you must declare a shark-jumping moment, the best bet is to say that the show jumped between the two "Who Shot Mr. Burns?" episodes. That's far enough along to cover most of the best episodes, but not so far that it includes some of the wilder plot lines.

Note: If a white person says something that doesn't seem to make sense and they slightly change the sound of their voice, chances are that they are quoting something from *The Simpsons.*

128 Avoiding Confrontation

When white people have a problem with someone they generally prefer a solution that does not require any face-to-face confrontation. White people really do hate a significant portion of the population, yet for some reason they are petrified of doing anything that might make someone hate them back. It is a strange paradox.

Normally when a white person has become frustrated with a person or situation they will choose to bottle up their rage and complain extensively to friends and relatives. It is the dream of every white person to be able to resolve all conflicts by complaining to unrelated parties. Because of this, white people are able to endure years of frustration and anger without saying a word in the hopes that everything will just work itself out without having to make a scene.

This concept can seem a bit complex and likely requires an example. One situation feared by white people is to find themselves near someone who is very talkative and friendly, be it at work, with a neighbor, or on an airplane. On the surface, it would seem as though a friendly, talkative person would be beloved by all, but this is simply not the case with white people. For the most part, white people only like talking to people they already know, and when this option is unavailable they prefer to listen to music, read, or pretend to be asleep. So when they find themselves having to pretend to be nice to a very outgoing person who bores them, they are in quite a pickle. They know that they cannot tell the person to shut up without being perceived as a jerk, so instead they rearrange their life and activities in an effort to avoid this person until their secret wishes for them to leave will come true. Sadly, they rarely do.

Generally, ignoring the problem is preferred by white people, but occasionally they will be pushed too far. When a white person reaches the breaking point, they will write a letter or an email to the person who has wronged them. The email will likely be well thought out and produced over the course of a few hours with many sentences apologizing for being in conflict. White people will say they prefer this method so that they can get their thoughts presented more clearly, but in reality it's just easier to avoid talking to someone. Once the email has been received and replied to, the healing process can begin and the friendship can resume.

This is essential knowledge if you ever find yourself in conflict with a white person. Do not confront them directly, as they will back down, agree to everything you say, and then immediately start talking about you to their friends, who will all turn on you. Direct confrontation is viewed by white people as a sign of instability, with the possibility that you might punch them. It is very difficult to recover from if you are not drunk at the time.

The best method is to wait as long as possible to see if the white person will send you the olive-branch email. If they don't, and you have reached your own breaking point, wait five more days and send it yourself. They will appreciate your utilization of the tested white method of conflict resolution.

 **DJs**

Within the world of white people, there might be no better job than DJ: knowing a lot about music; playing vinyl; no real musical talent required; and constant recognition of how great you are for knowing about music. It is perfect.

In the same way that every white person believes they would make a good photographer or writer, every single one believes that they would make a fantastic DJ. Because of this, white people have elevated DJs to the same status as actual musicians in the hopes that one day they can join the ranks.

Approximately 60 percent of white people will be in a band at some point in their lives, and the remaining 40 percent will attempt to be DJs. They generally follow the same trajectory. At first, they will choose a DJ name that will depend on the style of DJ they want to be. If they are really into hip-hop and want to be accepted into the community, they will likely choose a "thug" name like DJ AK-47 or DJ Gatz. If they love hip-hop but sort of understand that they are hopelessly white, they will choose a funny name like DJ Optimus Prime or DJ Snork. Once they have settled on a name they will begin by buying all sorts of hip-hop vinyl and putting together mix tapes for their friends with a lot of scratches to show their "technique." They will seek out only the most underground remixes and will likely produce a poor-quality "mashup"

in which they'll mix a hip-hop song with a pop instrumental.

By the time they reach college, the type-A DJ has morphed into the type-B DJ, and they have begun to experiment with pop songs and music from the '80s. Showing that they are into a diverse mix of music earns them much respect with the crowd, and being able to go from 50 Cent to Corey Hart shows their exceptional range and growth as a "musician."

After graduation, white people will continue to pursue this passion and will assemble a group of friends who love to see them "spin." White people prefer the word *spin* because it sounds cooler than "choosing songs for people to listen to."

Note: DJs have the best talent-to-groupie ratio of any career.

130 | Carbon Offsets

As much as white people would love to be able to do everything in an Earth-friendly way, the reality of their needs sometimes just doesn't match up to current environmental options. For example, when a white person needs to travel to India for a yoga retreat, they are going to have to get on a plane and in the process release tons of carbon dioxide into the air. Though simply avoiding air travel would be a good way to solve this, that's just not a fair thing to ask. Fortunately, there are carbon offsets.

A carbon offset occurs when a white person does something bad to the environment, like flying on an airplane or buying an SUV, and then simply gives some money to a company like TerraPass, which then plants a bunch of trees to make up for the infraction. In much the same way that Catholics sin and then ask forgiveness in confession, white people commit a sin and then just pay a bunch of money to remove the guilt. It is an astonishingly efficient system.

The system is also useful since white people can sit on a plane surrounded by other travelers, yet know deep down that they are saving the Earth while everyone else on the plane is destroying it—even though they are all on the same flight.

Since it is very difficult for white people to check up on the status of their carbon offsets, this is an excellent opportunity for personal financial gain. Whenever a white person says that they are going to take a flight, ask if they are paying for a carbon offset. If they say no, then you should introduce them to your new carbon-offset company, but be as unclear as possible about exactly how you will create the offset. Then buy yourself a Toyota Prius.

131

Following Their Dreams

White people are required to support anyone who decides to follow their dreams, regardless of the likelihood for success. This is one of the most important things you can ever learn.

Because white people generally do not have to worry about money in any serious way, or food, or shelter, or health care, their number-one concern is about the best way to make themselves happy. This eats up a tremendous amount of their time and has created many lucrative side industries, such as therapy, writer's workshops, acting classes, screenwriting software, and academia.

From a very young age, white people are told that the greatest thing they can do is to follow their dreams, and that they should not listen to anyone who tries to hold them back. Within white culture this law is about as unbreakable as gravity.

Generally a white person is most likely to follow their dream between the ages of 18 and 25. The majority will wait until they finish college before moving away to chase their dream of being an actor, writer, photographer, director, artist, musician, DJ, or producer.

If you meet a white person who has just finished college and has told you that they are moving to Brooklyn to become a writer, you should never under any circumstances suggest that they are making a mistake. When they are this young, it's best to say, "Of course, you have to take a chance now, because you may not have it when you are older. But I know you're going to make it." This last bit of encouragement will virtually guarantee a free place to stay when you visit New York City.

Do not feel bad for the white person or their parents. Following their dreams at this age is completely acceptable since failure will only really result in later acceptance to law school and perhaps a few sizeable loans from their parents. Depending on their degree and their parents, they will be able to catch up to their non-dream-following counterparts within five years. So supporting them at this stage is not really all that destructive.

However, some white people do *not* follow their dreams immediately out of college, and here is where the danger lies. As they begin to get older and feel disenchanted with their current job, they begin to think back to the dreams they had when they were younger. While it would seem logical that a real friend would say, "Hey, you just turned forty, do you really think it's a good idea to get your PhD in English? You know you won't get tenure until you're sixty, right?" nothing could be further from the truth.

Regardless of how catastrophic and irresponsible their actions are, if the end goal is to "follow their dreams" you must support them blindly or else you will be seen as a Simon Cowell–esque figure who is hated by all as a crusher of hope.

It is best to say something funny that also implies inevitable success, like "Can I be an extra when the movie gets made?" or "I expect a signed first edition!" It does not matter if you are lying.

Start

Do you like your job? —**NO**→ Do you like your industry? —**NO**→

↓ **YES**

Remain at job and wait for a promotion

↓ **YES**

Find a new job

Organic T-shirt company/ record label

Maternity clothing store ←**YES**— Is pregnancy beautiful? ←

↓ **NO**

Children's bookstore ←**Poorly read**— What is the bigger crime: Poorly read children or poorly dressed children?

↓ **Poorly dressed**

Children's clothing store

Breakfast-only restaurant

↑ **Breakfast**

Breakfast or lunch? ←**Savory**— Do you like things that are savory or sweet? ←

↓ **Lunch**

Sandwich shop

↓ **Sweet**

Organic bakery

If you encounter a white person who is experiencing professional malaise, use this chart to help give them advice about what to do with their lives.

Find cheap food (hamburger, macaroni and cheese), make it expensive and organic, and sell it at high prices

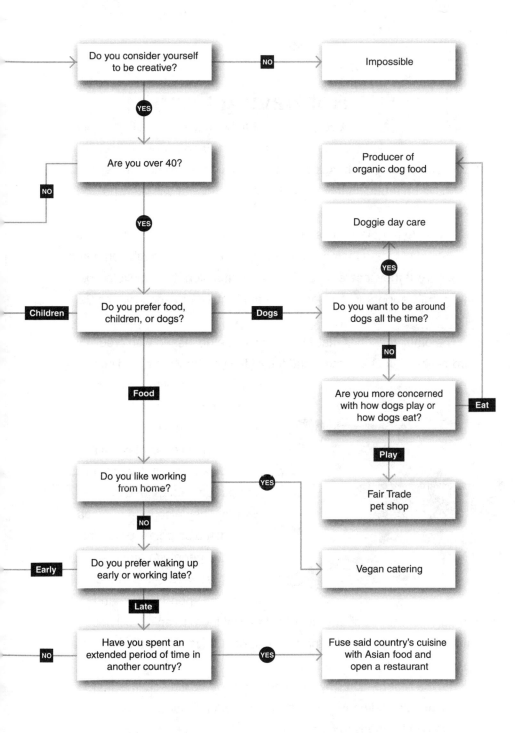

Do you consider yourself to be creative? → **NO** → Impossible

YES ↓

Are you over 40?

NO

YES ↓

Do you prefer food, children, or dogs? — **Children**

— **Dogs** → Do you want to be around dogs all the time?

YES ↑ Doggie day care

Producer of organic dog food

NO ↓

Are you more concerned with how dogs play or how dogs eat? — **Eat**

Play ↓

Food ↓

Do you like working from home? — **YES** →

NO ↓

Fair Trade pet shop

Do you prefer waking up early or working late? — **Early**

Vegan catering

Late ↓

Have you spent an extended period of time in another country? — **NO**

— **YES** → Fuse said country's cuisine with Asian food and open a restaurant

White
Career Guidance ?

132 | Not Having Cash

A very important thing to know about white people is that in spite of their considerable wealth, they hate to carry cash. Ask the nearest white person how much cash they have on them. If they are under 35, the answer will likely be under $10.

For white people cash leads to all sorts of problems. First, they are very afraid of losing their cash either by accident or through some kind of robbery. If they lose a credit card or get it stolen, they make a few phone calls and they can sleep easy at night. Not the case with a $20 bill.

The other reason is that white people are obsessed with credit card rewards. Just ask them and they'll tell you how their credit card

rewards them with airline miles, Amazon points, or even cash back. If they have to pay for something in cash, it just kills them to know that they are missing out on a chance to get rewards. They also hate pennies.

Cash also poses problems for white people in group settings. Because of the amount of time they spend in bars and restaurants, they need a system that allows them to split a bill accurately and fairly among the party. A pile of $20s is simply a shot in the dark.

But the real reason why white people have so little cash is that their schedules take them from home to work to sandwich shops to work to Whole Foods to home and then to bed. There is simply no time to stop at an ATM.

This information can be useful if you bring a white person to an ethnic restaurant that only takes cash. Never assume that white people will have money, and unless you want to give out a short-term loan, you should *always* tell a white person in advance if a restaurant is cash only.

133 | Adopting Foreign Children

Much as white people tend to prefer rescue dogs over purebreds, when it comes to children an increasing number of white people are turning to foreign countries. Africa and Asia are supplying the majority of these babies to white couples, who cannot wait to begin the journey of raising a foreign child.

On some levels, the foreign child is superior to the home-grown one, since the parents will always know that they took the child from a bad situation and brought him or her to a better one. This creates an important feeling of debt that will help to ensure the child remains loyal and obedient to the parents, something missing in many white children.

But the most important reason white parents are tripping over themselves for foreign babies is that they know it's their last chance to adopt another culture. When they chose to marry another white person, they gave up their opportunity to marry someone from a different race and culture. This essentially robbed them of their opportunity to learn a new language, a new cuisine, and a new wardrobe, and an excuse to repeatedly travel to a foreign country to "recharge." But a foreign child puts all of this right back into play!

White parents know that their role is not to merely assimilate the child and fool him or her into thinking that they are blood relatives. Instead, they must raise the child to be aware of his or her heritage and unique culture. For white parents this means new music! Language classes! Cooking classes! And at least a yearly trip to the child's homeland, with which the parents have formed a deep bond.

At dinner parties, playgrounds, and school functions the parents can now be experts on Vietnam or China or Sierra Leone. No amount of travel can compare to the expertise acquired by raising a child. Not even study abroad can trump this one.

If a white couple has adopted a child from your homeland, be prepared to have your culture thrown back at you with the force of a hurricane. In this situation it is advisable that you tell the parents what a great job they are doing keeping the child connected to his or her heritage. For extra credit, say that the child is more [insert country] than you were growing up. You will instantly jump to the top of any friend list.

The important thing to remember when you see a white couple with a foreign child is to ask about the country the child came from. They will have a very long and likely tragic story that should always end with you saying, "And now he/she is here with you. It's amazing how the world works itself out." Saying this means that you can count on the couple to give you a kidney if you should ever need one.

134 LEED Certification

Labels are important to white people. Organic labels on food help them determine what to eat, T-shirts are like body labels that help them determine who to date, Apple labels help them buy electronics, the McSweeney's label helps them determine what to read, and indie labels help to ensure quality in music. But what about buildings? How do you know if the building you are in has been made according to the exacting standards that you apply to your coffee? Thankfully, LEED has stepped in to help make sure that white people can even make their buildings feel superior.

LEED stands for Leadership in Energy and Environmental Design, which has emerged as the preeminent organization for setting energy and environmental standards for architecture and building construction. Architects who plan on serving a mostly white market can become LEED-accredited and immediately start selling

themselves as environmental architects. LEED architect is probably the most respected job (excluding any kind of artist) that a white person can have.

Buildings can also be retrofitted with changes to become LEED-certified, which essentially means that they are acceptable for white people to enter.

It is important to familiarize yourself with LEED standards so that if you are ever invited to a vegetarian's house for dinner and they start bugging you about the environmental impact of eating meat, you can ask them if their place is LEED-certified. "Oh, it's not? I would say those in a glass house shouldn't cast stones, but I think a glass house would be more energy efficient than this one."

135 | Expensive Strollers

To help prepare their children for a lifetime of driving expensive cars, white parents like to make sure that they are pushed around in the most expensive of European strollers. Though it could also be said that the lack of European luxury hybrids has forced white parents into using those funds to purchase the most expensive possible alternative-energy vehicle.

The energy is considered alternative since it comes from a nanny.

It is simply understood that strollers start at $800, and it is not wise to question this. In fact, it has been shown that white children who are pushed around in substandard strollers often grow up to be only marginally gifted.

The best thing you can do is to wait until a white person has had their second child. Find out when they are likely to stop needing the stroller and plan your first child around this event. A free stroller is a free stroller.

136 Singer-Songwriters

White people enjoy a variety of music, ranging from indie rock all the way to underground hip-hop, but of all musical performers, the top-ranked are usually singer-songwriters.

Singer-songwriters generally fall into two categories: guy with acoustic guitar or girl on piano. Sometimes there are exceptions, like Ani DiFranco (girl/guitar) or Rufus Wainwright (guy/piano), who are both very acceptable to white people and are safe to list as your favorite musician.

For the most part, singer-songwriters perform their own songs, which reflect their life experiences and observations on modern life in

New York City, Portland, or San Francisco. White people enjoy hearing about others who have gone through problems similar to theirs and like to try to match them to their own lives. For example, when a white person leaves for college, they like to listen to a song that talks about leaving something behind or is equally applicable to the situation. In this case "First Day of My Life" by Bright Eyes would be applicable, since it can be interpreted as the first day of college being like the first day of real life. This is also very common during difficult breakups.

WARNING: If you ever make a mix for someone, be careful not to put any songs by a singer-songwriter on there, because the recipient will attempt to interpret the lyrics in an effort to uncover your true feelings. Then things will get weird. Best to stick with the Kinks.

137 Eating Outside

It is a rule in white culture that if something is done outside, it is vastly improved. Reading, working, and holding a philosophy class are activities that are significantly improved by being done outside. But nothing sees a more significant boost in enjoyment by venturing outdoors than eating.

Picnics and cookouts have been a staple of white culture for years. When these activities involve groups, they essentially function as an outdoor dinner party offering a whole new set of things to judge, like patio furniture, themed alcohol, and quality of food.

But nothing excites white people more than restaurant patios. Of course, there are many different types of outdoor dining options, and it's important to be aware of the major differences. For breakfast and

lunch, white people generally embrace the sidewalk café. This enables them to enjoy the day, show off to passersby, and, even if only for a minute, pretend they are in Europe. Few better things can be said in one of these situations than "This reminds me of a delightful place I used to go to in France."

When day turns to night, the cafés are replaced by patios. White people will base their entire evening around trying to figure out which bar has the best patio scene. In fact, after '80s night, there may be no better white activity than drinking in an outdoor bar.

However, as much as white people love being outside, they also hate slight discomfort. So when eating in a café make sure that the white person you are with has appropriate levels of shade. If the sun moves significantly during the course of your meal they will likely ask to leave. It is not a good idea to say, "If you like shade so much, there's this entire place called 'inside' that has nothing but shade." Later at night, you might notice steel obelisks that sort of look like little umbrellas; these are propane heaters. They allow white people to enjoy the temperature control of an indoor environment without the heating and energy efficiency traditionally associated with being inside. Again, it is not a good idea to question why white people do this.

138 Books

The role of books in white culture is perhaps as important as organic food—essential for survival. However, understand that this is not about literacy or reading, but about the physical object of a book.

Try this out as an experiment. Show a white person a photo of a living room that features an entire wall of floor-to-ceiling bookshelves. They are guaranteed to respond by saying how much they would love that for their own home and that they are planning on having a living room just like that in the future.

This is because white people need to show off the books that they have read. Just as hunters will mount the heads of their kills, white people need to let people know that they have made their way through hundreds or even thousands of books. After all, what's the point of reading a book if people don't know you've read it? It's like a tree falling in the forest.

As much as white people do not want you rifling through their medicine cabinet, they are desperate for you to examine their bookshelves. When scanning through the rows of books, the best things you can say are "You made it through *Infinite Jest*? Wow" or "I didn't know you loved Joyce so much." If your intentions are to grow your friendship either romantically or platonically, there is no better technique than to ask to borrow one of the books.

This is because lending out books is the only practical reason for white people to hold on to their entire collection. So by asking to borrow a copy, you are justifying their decision to save the book, allowing them to both introduce you to a new author and assert their status as a well-read individual. It is the perfect move.

But there are times when your visit to a white person's house is not long enough for a full inspection of their bookshelves. How then can you gauge their taste? Simple, just look at the coffee table. You see, white people like to purchase very expensive, very large books that they can put on their coffee tables for other people to see and then use to make value judgments. If the coffee-table book is about art, then the white person wants you to ask them about their trip to the Tate Modern. If it's about photography, they want you to ask them about their new camera. If it's about football or bikinis, you should politely ask to leave.

So now that you know white people like books, you might assume that a book is the perfect gift. Not so fast. There are a few possible outcomes from giving books, and few of them end well. If you get a white person a book that they already have, the situation will be uncomfortable. If you get them a book that they do not want, you will be forever viewed as someone with poor taste in literature. In the event that you get them a book that they want and do not have, they are forced to recognize that they have not read it, which instantly paints you as a threat. There is no way to win when you give a book to a white person.

 # Music Festivals

Imagine spending three days in a tent, but instead of being surrounded by nature you are surrounded by mud, oppressive heat, loudspeakers, and thousands of white people swaying with their eyes closed. Many people would call this "hell," "a nightmare that won't end," or "some sort of sci-fi zombie scenario that is worse than anything we could ever imagine." White people call this a "music festival" and will pay large amounts of money for the experience.

These events play an important part in white culture, as they provide both an excuse for travel and an excuse for using outrageous amounts of recreational drugs. If a white person tells you that they are going to a music festival, push a little further into their plans and you will discover that they have spent weeks acquiring different drugs and doing Internet research to find out how to best combine them. They will also be happy to tell you their exact inventory: "We got four hits of Ecstasy, an ounce of 'shrooms, an  ounce of weed, an eight ball of coke, ten hits of blotter acid, all sorts of pills, and some GHB to help come down. I think it should be enough."

These drugs are necessary because the sheer size of the festival means that the majority of people in attendance will be watching everything on large screens near the stage. So, to make that clear, white people are paying for the right to watch large televisions with other white people through obnoxiously loud speakers.

Before you start talking to anyone about a music festival you have to understand that your choice of festival defines the type of white person that you are. Type A people who regularly attend festivals like Glastonbury or Roskilde are more into European music, which often means electronic. They will be bringing more Ecstasy to the show. Type B people attend Bonnaroo and are into jam bands and will likely have beards, sandals, and an abundance of psychedelic mushrooms and acid. Type C people prefer Coachella and are passionate about indie rock; they will likely be bringing antidepressants and water bottles to the event. It is acceptable to confuse types A and C but *never* confuse type B with type A or C. Everyone will be offended.

Do not under any circumstances attend one of these festivals.

140   Glasses

As white people get older they attempt to construct their "look" much in the same way they construct a Mii avatar on the Nintendo Wii. Since many white people look alike, they are desperate to find ways to have a distinctive look. Some try complex facial hair or wild haircuts, but these require rather

long-term commitments and are not always welcome at nonprofit organizations or film-festival offices. The easiest way for a white person to express their individuality and uniqueness is through their choice of glasses.

Aren't there white people who don't wear glasses? You might have to double-check that they are the right kind of white people. Or it must just be a "contact day," which white people are permitted to have from time to time.

The right choice of eyewear can tell the world that you are well read (your eyes have deteriorated from too many late nights at the library), have good taste in music, and do not care that the world perceives you as a nerd. Because of this, white people need to find glasses that are rare and unique, but at the same time made of thick plastic frames in either black or brown. These strong frames force people to recognize that the white person is wearing glasses and to acknowledge their intelligence. Glasses that appear invisible, or at least are not prominent, are seen as inferior, since they do not demand recognition and often blend in with the face.

Because of the relative difficulty in finding such a unique item, it is never a good idea to ask a white person where they got their glasses. This is because they are extremely fearful of other white people wearing the same kind. It's hard to describe how much of a big deal this is.

There used to be stories about how primitive tribes would not allow photographs, which they feared would steal their souls. Well, when another white person buys and wears your style of glasses, it's sort of the same thing.

If you are ever searching for a neutral compliment for a white person, it's always a good idea to say, "I like your glasses." This will make them feel great about themselves, but won't make them feel as though you are hitting on them.

141 McSweeney's

McSweeney's is one of the most powerful forces in white culture. It is a literary magazine–publishing house that is so powerful that just knowing about it (not even reading it) is enough to gain the respect of white people.

It was founded in 1998 by white-person hero Dave Eggers as a literary magazine that only published work that had been rejected by other publications. It became very popular very quickly and soon expanded into multiple magazines, DVD magazines, and a publishing division.

There is a steady group of writers who regularly contribute to the magazine and eventually write books for the imprint. These writers form a very special crew, and are all very respected within the white community. Some are more successful than others, and they don't let just anybody into the group. In fact, it's sort of like the Wu-Tang Clan for white people.

In the same way that Method Man or the RZA can act in movies and release solo albums without taking away from their affiliation with the group, many McSweeney's writers are able to do solo projects away from the core group. This includes some who are regular contributors to NPR (Sarah Vowell) and *The Daily Show* (John Hodgman). Aside from Eggers, these are considered to be ultimate-level white people who set the standard for the rest of the community.

There are a number of ways to use this information. First, being able to discuss something you read in *McSweeney's* is considered highly desirable in both a friend and a mate. But there remains a move in white culture so unprecedented and powerful that only a few have dared attempt it. You see, *McSweeney's* is a very expensive magazine and does not lend itself well to gift subscriptions. But if you can afford the expense, a gift subscription to *McSweeney's* is a finishing move in your pursuit of white friendship. Even if it's only for one year, you have bought yourself a year of favors, rides, and free dinners.

 # Hardwood Floors

When white people envision their perfect home, it always has hardwood floors. In fact, most white people would prefer a dirt floor over wall-to-wall carpeting, because to them it would have the same level of cleanliness and probably fewer germs.

White people are petrified of germs, and when they look at a carpet all they can see is everything that has ever been spilled, tracked in, or shaken loose into the carpet fibers. But more disgusting to white people is that wall-to-wall carpeting reminds them of suburban homes, motel rooms, and the horrible apartments that they have visited or lived in over the years. It has no soul. Only germs.

Hardwood floors, on the other hand, are easily cleaned and give a sense of character to a place, since they are often the original flooring in older buildings. It is a well-known white fantasy to purchase a home

or apartment that has disgusting carpet
and then to pull it up to reveal a beautiful hardwood floor underneath. If you
can tell a similar story to white people it
will give them hope that they can one
day find a run-down home and turn it
into a modern masterpiece of interior
design. This is highly recommended.

Oddly enough, in spite of their hatred for wall-to-wall carpeting, white
people all love rugs.

143 Bakeries

If you're driving through an empty neighborhood
at night and need to determine if it's a white
neighborhood, the fastest way to do so is to look for a fancy bakery.
The presence of one such bakery signifies that you are in a rapidly
gentrifying white neighborhood, while two means you likely cannot afford a place there, and three means that it is safe for white children.

Using the finest organic ingredients and offering both gluten-free
and vegan alternatives, the modern bakery has come to define the
white neighborhood. It is a source of pride, inspiration, and cupcakes.

When a white person brings a dessert from their local bakery to a
dinner party, they are doing much more than just bringing food. They
are bringing their neighborhood, their newly renovated home, and their
sense of superiority. Bringing a delicious local treat says "Look at me,
look at what my neighborhood produces. It's organic, it's authentic, it's
delicious, it's all that is me. Did you get those cookies at Costco?"

The bakery also inspires hope in white people. Many of them
dream of quitting their 9 to 5 job and opening a small bakery within
walking distance of their home. In this little shop they will listen to ex-

cellent music and provide the community with the proper nourishment to help fight childhood obesity and raise property values.

Buying local certainly has the most significance for white people, but that does not mean that they won't travel great distances to seek out new and exciting food. Knowing where to get the best cookie, French bread, or macaroon is of critical importance among white people, and being able to tell someone where to get the "best cupcake in the city" is considered an essential element in being an expert on local food. However, attempting to tell someone about a bakery that is no longer considered "cutting edge" will result in mockery that might last for months and possibly a year. To put it into context, that would be like telling someone about a great new Irish band called "U2."

Modern Art Museums

The majority of travel done by white people is justified by their need to find themselves or, occasionally, to serve in some sort of charity project. But when white people take a trip for pleasure they are required to visit a modern art museum.

Nothing justifies a visit to New York or London more than the promise of a visit to MoMA or the Tate Modern. So much so, in fact, that if a white person travels to the UK for seven days and visits an art museum on the first and then spends the next six watching television in their room, the trip is considered to be a cultural success.

But what about regular art galleries or museums? Except in the case of parents with very young children, these are regarded as tourist destinations reserved for the wrong kind of white people. Returning home from Paris and declaring you saw the Mona Lisa is met with the same level of respect as returning home from McDonald's and declaring that you ate a cheeseburger. These museums are filled with sculptures and paintings of mostly religious artwork and gaudy gold painted frames that would look terrible next to designer furniture. That's right, white people love modern art because it fits in better with their furniture. Simple as that.

Though few can afford well-known artists, white people harbor dreams of somehow being able to afford the work of young artists before they become famous. This is the same way they feel about indie rock. But unlike music, buying into the right young artist will yield both respect and financial gain, perhaps the two things most beloved by white people (see #73, Gentrification, for further evidence).

But again, even the practice of buying actual art will elude many young white people. So they are left with only one recourse: the gift shop. A white person in a modern art museum gift shop is not comparable to a kid in a candy store. They're more like a drug addict in the evidence room.

Prints, art supplies, T-shirts, posters, books, postcards, knick-knacks—it's an entire room devoted to a collection of things that serve as evidence of both good taste and a visit to the museum. If you are in a city with a well-known modern art museum, you can literally buy *anything* from the gift shop and a white person will love it. No other retail chain, not even IKEA, can offer that kind of security.

Cheese

Wine and cheese are a great pairing for any white event: dinner party, gallery opening, or presidential-debate party. But, as with all things, white people are expected to have an extensive and deep knowledge of cheese, cheese regions, and proper cheese pairings.

The uses for cheese in white culture are almost limitless. It is an important part of any expensive sandwich, an essential hors d'oeuvre, and a required salad topping. Knowing your way around a cheese plate can help to improve your standing with white people in an instant. But professing a love for the wrong kind of cheese will quickly paint you as the wrong kind of person.

Anything presliced is unacceptable, anything manufactured by a major dairy producer is unacceptable, and even being aware of "American cheese" is considered highly problematic.

It is best to treat cheese like indie music in so much as it's best to like cheeses that no one has ever heard of. Also, it's a very good idea to have obscure alternative cheeses for common food situations. For example, if a white person says, "I love fresh Parmesan grated on my gnocchi," you should reply, "Even if it's authentic Parmesan, I really think a pecorino is just so much nicer. It adds a nuttiness that you don't find in common Parmesans." This is also effective when talking about grilled cheese sandwiches.

These adjectives are commonly recognized as the best for cheese: *nutty, sharp,* and *rich. Smoky* can go either way and is best avoided.

If you are planning on hosting an event with white people, it's a good idea to head over to a gourmet store and visit its cheese section (don't worry, they have them). Ask the cheese guy to recommend a plate. Take notes on what he says, then repeat at party to a rapt audience. If you are able to introduce a white person to a new cheese, it's like introducing them to a future spouse. They will remember it forever, or at least until they get bored.

Therapy

Before an explanation of therapy, it is essential to explain a few key principles about how white people operate.

First, any time that a white person succeeds it is entirely because of their hard work and natural talent. It may take a few questions to get them to admit this, but trust me, they all believe it. They will tell you how they worked hard in high school to get into college, worked hard in college to get a good internship, and have been busting their ass for years to hold their current position. No one gave them a free ride, they earned it.

On the other end of the spectrum, every single white failure can be attributed to parents.

Because of this split, an entire industry known as "therapy" has popped up to help white people try to turn those failures into successes.

A therapist is a person who listens to white problems and basically promises not to tell anybody else, like the friend all white people wish they had but know they don't. This therapist will meet with a white person one to five times a week depending on the severity of the problems.

During the session they will ask questions and allow the white person to vent all the problems they are having with relationships, jobs, and family. When the allotted time is up, the white person will pay and then return to their life.

On the surface, you may think this is something to be ashamed of and you should never ask a white person about therapy. However, all white people require therapy. The only difference among them is that some are still waiting to begin. It is perfectly normal to see a therapist, and white people are very comfortable talking about how they are undoing the damage done by their parents.

It is *not* recommended that you ask white people what they talk about in therapy. This is not because of the personal nature of the conversations, but rather because they could start to see you as a free alternative who might be able to deliver ethnic wisdom.

Public Transportation That Is Not a Bus

When white people talk about their favorite things about New York City, they will almost always mention the subway. They will go on and on about how they were able to get from their hotel to the restaurant to their friend's place without a car. Most likely the conversation will continue with them talking about how jealous they are of people in New York who don't have to drive.

White people all support the idea of public transportation and will be happy to tell you about how subways and streetcars/trams have helped to energize cities like Chicago and Portland. They will tell you all about the energy and cost savings of having people abandon their cars for public transportation and how they hope that one day they can live in a city where they will be car-free.

At this point, you are probably thinking about the massive number of buses that serve your city and how you have never seen a white person riding them. To a white person a bus is essentially a giant mini-van that continually stops to pick up progressively smellier people. You should never, ever point this out to a white person. It will make them recognize that they might not love public transporta-tion as much as they thought, and then they will feel sad.

When it comes to the subject it's best to understand that white people do not recognize public transit as a viable option until a subway line is built that runs directly from their house to their work. Until that time, public transportation is a luxury only for New Yorkers and Europeans, sort of like opera.

148   Dive Bars

For white people who do not like to dance, a local dive bar is acknowledged as the best place to spend a night out. For those of you who don't know, a dive bar is a place with cheap drinks and minimal decoration that was formerly fre-quented by those who dislike white people.

The dive bar is a treasure trove of authenticity: authentic people, authentic light beer, authentic urinals, authentic beer mirrors, and au-thentic imitation red leather on the furniture. In spite of their love of in-terior design and modern furniture, and their taste in art, white people cannot get enough of the dive-bar atmosphere. This is because white people like to believe that they are still working class, or at the very least able to relate to the noble proletariat that frequents a dive bar.

A common fantasy is for a white person to "discover" a dive bar and quickly become a fixture at the place so that the regulars will accept them as one of their own. Of course, one of the defining features of a good dive bar is that the locals actually hate the white people who frequent the bar. This is something that will become more and more pronounced as the bar and the neighborhood evolve.

After white people have found a good dive bar they begin to operate much like parasites. Soon they bring some friends, who bring  some friends, who bring some friends, and eventually the sleepy bar that served Miller Lite on tap now stocks Stella and is packed with people wearing scarves and glasses and complaining about how much they hate nightclubs.

By now, all of the original locals have moved on from both the bar and the neighborhood. If all goes according to plan, a few locals will remain and the original white person to discover the bar will feel proud to complain that this once great bar has changed for the worse.

If you are one of the remaining locals, there are some great opportunities for you to help compensate for the loss of your bar. First, that original white person will always buy you a drink if you ask for one to toast "the good old days." But don't think the gravy train stops there. The new white people in the bar will be desperate to distance themselves from their friends and prove that they are local, and there is no better way to do this than to befriend you. Once you know their names, just say hi anytime they enter the bar and you will drink for free for as long as you like.

149 Self-Importance

Implied but not stated in virtually every entry here is the notion of self-importance. Magically, over the past half century white people have been able to mask much of this self-importance through the arts, charities, nonprofit organizations, nongovernmental organizations, and childbirth.

The life of every white person is worthy of a memoir. Being born into a middle-class existence, having some difficult experiences in college, and taking a year off to teach in Asia/work in the Peace Corps/volunteer with Teach for America are all life stories realized only by a select few. Unfortunately, the publishing industry can only put out so many books each year and white people have had to turn to an alternative means: blogging.

Due to an undying need to share their life story with everyone who will listen, white people have taken to blogging in massive numbers, though it is no surprise that many have simply turned their journals/diaries into blogs where they talk about the latest episode of *American Idol,* Darfur, their experience at a coffee shop, and their concerns about the future. These were to be expected.

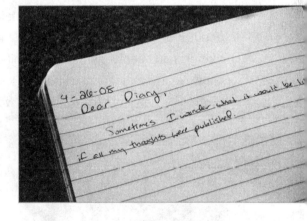

What has been less expected is the need for white people to document in blog format any experience that takes more than a week. Pregnancy, vacations to Asia and South America, renovations, child rearing, and car restoration have all become blogs that encourage the rest of the world to take notice of the astute observations and talent of the undiscovered writer.

When a white person shares their URL with you, do not say, "Do I have to read this now?" Instead, you should say, "I'd love to check it out," quickly read one post near the middle of the blog, and return to the white person, saying, "Oh man, I saw that post on [insert topic]. It was great. I forwarded it to all my friends." Doing this shows that you believe their life to be important and their presentation of that life to be worth your time. Sadly, the temporary boost in self-esteem for the white person is the only benefit to be gained from the blog and your interaction with it.

150 Rock Climbing

For much of human history, when a human being saw a mountain in front of them, their reaction was "Damn, I wish this mountain wasn't here, why can't someone just blow a hole through this?" One day, after many roads and tunnels had been constructed, a white person thought to himself, "You know what? I'm going to climb this, look around, then climb back down. The view from the top will be worth risking my life." And rock climbing was born.

Though the entire activity can be made pointless with the introduction of an extremely long ladder, white people love rock climbing almost more than they love camping. This is because the activity affords them the opportunity to be outside, to use a carabiner for something other than their keys, and to purchase a whole new set of expensive activity-specific clothing and accessories.

The appeal of the sport has grown in recent years as cities and college campuses have opened indoor rock-climbing facilities. Now urban white people can experience all the thrill of climbing up something, looking around, and then climbing back down without having to take a long drive—which is the only goal of rock climbing. There is no gold at the top of the mountain, no secret lair, not even a snack bar. The only reward is self-satisfaction and the opportunity to say, "Dude, crazy weekend. We did the summit of [insert mountain], it was intense. Me and a few buddies are planning a trip to Peru to climb."

Exploiting a person who is into rock climbing is not very difficult. Simply praise them for their tremendous skill and drop a hint that you would be willing to house-sit the next time they go climbing. (Note: House-sitting is the activity of living in a white person's house when they are away. It is a good opportunity to eat their food and make a few extra dollars.)

But how can you tell if a white person is into rock climbing? It's easy! Talk to them for ten minutes. White people who like rock climbing love to tell people about how they like to go "climbing" on the weekend and would like nothing more than for you to join them or at least enroll in a rock-climbing class. Do not accept.

How White Are You?

Check off everything that you like. When you're finished, count everything up and determine your whiteness percentage.

- [ ] 1 Coffee
- [ ] 2 Religions Their Parents Don't Belong To
- [ ] 3 Film Festivals
- [ ] 4 Assists
- [ ] 5 Farmer's Markets
- [ ] 6 Organic Food
- [ ] 7 Diversity
- [ ] 8 Barack Obama
- [ ] 9 Making You Feel Bad for Not Going Outside
- [ ] 10 Wes Anderson Movies
- [ ] 11 Asian Girls
- [ ] 12 Nonprofit Organizations
- [ ] 13 Tea
- [ ] 14 Having Black Friends
- [ ] 15 Yoga
- [ ] 16 Gifted Children
- [ ] 17 Hating Their Parents

- [ ] 18 Awareness
- [ ] 19 International Travel
- [ ] 20 Being an Expert on *Your* Culture
- [ ] 21 Writer's Workshops
- [ ] 22 Having Two Last Names
- [ ] 23 Microbreweries
- [ ] 24 Wine
- [ ] 25 David Sedaris
- [ ] 26 Manhattan (and Now Brooklyn, Too!)
- [ ] 27 Marathons
- [ ] 28 Not Having a TV
- [ ] 29 '80s Night
- [ ] 30 Wrigley Field
- [ ] 31 Snowboarding
- [ ] 32 Veganism/Vegetarianism
- [ ] 33 Marijuana
- [ ] 34 Architecture
- [ ] 35 *The Daily Show with Jon Stewart/The Colbert Report*
- [ ] 36 Brunch
- [ ] 37 Renovations
- [ ] 38 *Arrested Development*
- [ ] 39 Netflix
- [ ] 40 Apple Products
- [ ] 41 Indie Music
- [ ] 42 Sushi

☐ 93 Rugby

☐ 94 New Balance Shoes

☐ 95 Beards

☐ 96 Having Children in Their Late Thirties

☐ 97 Red Hair

☐ 98 Noam Chomsky

☐ 99 Non-Motorized Boating

☐ 100 The Boston Red Sox

☐ 101 Scarves

☐ 102 Cleanses

☐ 103 Self-Deprecating Humor

☐ 104 Integrity

☐ 105 Pretending to Be a Canadian When Traveling Abroad

☐ 106 The Criterion collection

☐ 107 Natural Childbirth

☐ 108 High School English Teachers

☐ 109 Native Wisdom

☐ 110 Trying Too Hard

☐ 111 Portland, Oregon

☐ 112 Free Health Care

☐ 113 Che Guevera

☐ 114 *The New Yorker*

☐ 115 Non-American News Sources

☐ 116 Subtitles

☐ 117 Premium Juice

☐ **143 Bakeries**

☐ **144 Modern Art Museums**

☐ **145 Cheese**

☐ **146 Therapy**

☐ **147 Public Transportation That Is Not a Bus**

☐ **148 Dive Bars**

☐ **149 Self-Importance**

☐ **150 Rock Climbing**

_____ ÷ **150 =** _____%
  TOTAL

Guide

15	=	10% white
30	=	20% white
45	=	30% white
60	=	40% white
75	=	50% white
90	=	60% white
105	=	70% white
120	=	80% white
135	=	90% white
150	=	100% white

Acknowledgments

I want to thank my wife, Jessica Lander, for her love and support; my father, Richard, for giving me a sense of humor; my brother, Aaron, for pointing out my pretentiousness; and my three universities for the inspiration.

I would also like to thank Myles Valentin for his inspiration and brillance in writing about Asian Girls and Oscar Parties.

Photograph Acknowledgments

The numbers listed below refer to the entries (e.g., #1 is Coffee).

iStockphoto®: 3, 4, 8, 9, 11, 12, 14, 15, 16, 17, 18, 19, 21, 22, 25, 26, 29, 30, 31, 33, 37, 38, 39, 41, 43, 44, 45, 47, 50, 51, 52, 56, 57, 59, 62, 65, 66, 67, 68, 69, 72, 73, 74, 76, 77, 78, 80, 81, 83, 85, 86, 88, 89, 90, 91, 92, 93, 96, 97, 98, 99, 100, 101, 102, 103, 104, 105, 106, 107, 108, 109, 110, 111, 112, 113, 114, 116, 118, 119, 120, 122, 123, 124, 126, 129, 130, 131, 132, 133, 134, 135, 136, 138, 139, 141, 142, 144, 146, 147, 148, 150

Jess Lander: title-page spread, 1, 2, 5, 6, 7, 10, 13, 20, 23, 24, 28, 32, 34, 35, 36, 40, 42, 46, 48, 49, 53, 54, 55, 58, 60, 61, 63, 64, 71, 75, 79, 82, 84, 87, 94, 95, 115, 117, 121, 125, 127, 128, 137, 140, 143, 145, 149

Rebecca Shapiro: 27

Jill Schwartzman: 70

About the Author

CHRISTIAN LANDER is the creator of the
website Stuff White People Like. He is
a PhD dropout who was the 2006 public
speaking instructor of the year at Indiana
University. He has lived in Toronto,
Montreal, Copenhagen, Tucson, Indiana,
and now Los Angeles, where he lives with
his wife, Jess, a photographer who contributed many of the photos in the book.

About the Type

This book was set in Helvetica, a typeface created in 1957 by Max Miedinger and Eduard Hoffman at the Haas'sche Schriftgiesserei, a type foundry in Münchenstein, Switzerland. It has become the official font of white people. Whenever a white person opens a store or restaurant they must create a sign that uses Helvetica, justified bottom right or left. They love it so much they even made a documentary (see #57) about it.